Voices on the Green

Voices on the Green

DOROTHY CLEAL

ISIS
LARGE PRINT
Oxford

First published in Great Britain 2005
by
ISIS Publishing Ltd.

Published in Large Print 2005 by ISIS Publishing Ltd.,
7 Centremead, Osney Mead, Oxford OX2 0ES
by arrangement with
the Author

British Library Cataloguing in Publication Data
Cleal, Dorothy
    Voices on the green. – Large print ed.
    (Isis reminiscence series)
    1. Cleal, Dorothy – Childhood and youth
    2. Large type books
    3. Great Britain – Social life and
    customs – 1918–1945
    4. England, South East – Biography
    I. Title
    942.2'083'092

ISBN 0–7531–9326–4 (hb)
ISBN 0–7531–9327–2 (pb)

Printed and bound in Great Britain by
T. J. International Ltd., Padstow, Cornwall

For Mary,
who made the sun shine

CONTENTS

1. A Foreign Country 1

2. Early Voices 31

3. Green People 65

4. Tumbledown Dick's 90

5. A Growing Summer 139

6. Pigotts 154

7. Over the River 186

CHAPTER
ONE

A Foreign Country

"The past is a foreign country. They do things differently there."
                                          L. P. Hartley

In the beginning, there was light, and my earliest recollection of what "light" meant was the yellow strip shining in the darkness beneath the door which led from the bedroom (we had only one) into the living room/ kitchen, and with the light came the comforting knowledge that my mother was only a few steps away, and that one call would bring her in, dispelling darkness and nightmares, dispensing love and reassurance and handkerchiefs and drinks of water. My early brush with death had made her more lenient with me than with my much worthier older sister, who was incapable of cunning; but she loved my sister best, and rightly so.

I was born in an Army hut on a dark November day almost exactly six years after the end of the Great War (that's what they called it then). I was a Scorpio, born between fire and water. Such a beginning should surely have presaged a lifetime of dramatic happenings, and made me a darkly colourful personality, but it did neither.

First, the Army hut. It was not, at the time of my birth, actually occupied by the Army. They had packed up and gone on that other November day six years earlier, when the guns fell silent — forever, people said, but by the time I was born they were already beginning to say other things. But at the end of the war it had seemed unlikely that there was a future for munitions factories. In the precincts of one such factory, improbably sited amid Hertfordshire cornfields and now in the process of conversion, my parents had taken up residence in November 1919, coming out of London shortly after their marriage because my father's doctor had recommended country air. My father had been in and out of hospital for the best part of a year following four years of war, half of which he had spent in a succession of prison camps, including one particularly brutal.

Among the friendships forged in that grim foundry was one between my father and a Scottish officer who, when they parted, had instructed him to get in touch if he had difficulty in getting a job when he was demobbed. Partly disabled and with the labour market flooded with returning servicemen, my father was glad to take up the offer, and it was his good luck that the job thus offered was in the country and provided accommodation — of a sort; but he and my mother were in no position to look a gift horse in the mouth. So, newly married, they came into Hertfordshire, and I loved my mother's description of the pair of them standing at Ware station in the rain, that long-ago November day, waiting for the pony and trap which was to take them the remaining few miles, my mother in her "Merry Widow" hat (my father's description — though surely a real "Merry Widow" would have been out of date by 1919?). My mother recalled how conspicuous she had felt, clutching an aspidistra in a highly-coloured art pot which had been a wedding present from Dad's sister Liz.

And so they came to what was to be home to them for the next nine years. I wonder whether my mother's heart sank when she saw the Army hut and the factory wall beyond. My father was, most of the time, an incurable optimist, and had no doubt painted a rosier picture than the facts warranted. But I suppose she knew him well enough by then to make allowances. At any rate, she always spoke as though their homecoming had been a happy one, and perhaps it was.

They settled in, contentedly enough, I think. Both had had hard lives and had known real poverty, so their fairly basic lifestyle wouldn't have worried them. They seem to have cared deeply for each other. My father, certainly, was "in love". (Strange to think of one's parents having a relationship of their own before they were one's parents.)

My sister Mary was born in the sweltering June of 1921, a great joy to them both. I arrived three and a half years later. I'm sure my father badly wanted a boy, for he himself was the only surviving son in a family of girls. It says much for him that he never gave the slightest indication of this, and loved me dearly.

My mother said in later years that I was made of bread and jam, for that was all she could eat when she was expecting me. She blamed herself afterwards because I was a pale, skinny child who looked likely to die young. (Much store was set in those days on the "bonniness" of babies; it was the ambition of mothers to have their offspring looking as much as possible like the baby on the "Cow and Gate" tins.) Despite this, I gather that I came into the world with great enthusiasm — too great for my poor mother's comfort. My father summoned the District Nurse, who arrived breathless after a three-mile bicycle ride in the grey dawn, just in time to grab me, and she said, "This one's got more vitality than your Mary." My apparent frailty was misleading. But Mary had more character, and my famous vitality didn't last beyond my teens.

Our garden ran down to a little paddock where we kept a few chickens and a goat, and beyond that was a stream — indeed, a river, for it was deep enough to drown in and had a name. In winter it became brown and swollen with the water draining off the fields, and sometimes, after a long wet spell, it would overflow its banks and come up over the low-lying meadows. This happened quite dramatically on the day I was born, and the water crept up at an alarming rate, even threatening the house itself. At the same time, some high-spirited local lads, looking for something to brighten a dull Saturday in the manner of high-spirited lads everywhere, had set fire to a hayrick just across the lane, and with the wind coming from that direction, the house and factory stood in the path of the flying sparks. It would have been threatening enough in the ordinary way, but the factory, having fulfilled its wartime rôle, had been

4

converted, ploughshare-wise, into a producer of Christmas crackers, and there was still a magazine containing explosive material somewhere beyond the wall against which our bungalow stood. The danger was considered real enough and plans were afoot to move us out when the wind changed and the danger was averted. At roughly the same time, the overflowing river reached its limits, and that danger passed also. The efficacy of my mother's prayers was something to be wondered at.

My birth left her with a weak heart — perhaps not surprisingly! She told me in later years that she thought she would die, and worried about leaving us motherless. The doctor could do nothing for her except to advise rest — not easy for a working-class mother in the 1920s. She dosed herself with Iron Jelloids and gradually got stronger. And despite a hard life with long periods of deprivation, she lived into her mid-eighties, surviving my father by many years. It was indeed her heart that finally let her down, but it had done sterling service, and so it should have, for it was one of the best.

Loving parent though she was to my sister and me, my mother didn't exactly "love children". She came from a family of ten herself, and had no illusions.

I don't think her own mother was very keen either. Her whole life must have been drudgery and grinding poverty; yet she remained lively to the end, never lost her zest for living nor her interest in what was going on in the world, and she was dearly loved by all her descendants. As I remember her, she was the perfect picture of a granny, a little rosy apple of a woman, toothless for nearly all her adult life, I think (as were almost all the working-class women above middle age in my early childhood). I hardly ever saw her without an apron almost reaching down to her tiny black boots, and in my mind's eye I see her now, clutching her little brown teapot on her way to empty the tea-leaves on the roses, whistling softly through her gums. She was very deaf, whistling away happily throughout the conversation of others, stopping here and there to beam at the speaker but quite oblivious to what was being said.

But this cosy picture doesn't tell the whole story. She claimed to be a "proper Cockney", born within the sound of Bow bells, but she was brought up at Kingston-on-Thames. Her father had died young. Her mother had worked for Mrs Edgar (of Swan and Edgar in Piccadilly), and this lady kindly set up the young widow in a washing establishment in Kingston. This was rather grandly referred to by my grandmother as a "laundry", but its size may be judged by Gran's memory of being stood on a stool at the age of four to wash the socks.

My mother had no recollection of ever seeing her maternal grandmother, and I don't know what became of her — though she remarried and had other children whom I met once or twice when very young. The only glimpse of her which has come down to me is in an incident reported by my grandmother. Coming out of church one Sunday, Gran was smiled at by a soldier, which earned her a slap round the face from her mother.

An apparently strict upbringing didn't do Gran a lot of good. At some time — at quite an early age — she was seduced by a member of the upper classes, and as a result gave birth to my uncle Jack. The seducer was (according to what she told my mother and no-one else — in an untypically confiding mood) a well-known actor, who moved in the highest social circles and was a friend of Lily Langtry. I don't know how the seduction came about, if true. Perhaps he was a house guest at one of the stately homes of the period and she was a servant; such encounters were not unknown.

Eventually she met and married my grandfather, who was also in service — a gardener for all the time I knew him, but as they seem to have met in London (where he spent his free time, such as it was, at the British Museum; not, one would think, a common pastime for a domestic servant), he may at that time have been a groom or coachman. That would explain his crippled leg, said to have been caused by a kick from a horse and permanently damaged because it was never treated.

They moved to his home village on the Oxford/Bucks border, and there my mother and the older children were born.

My grandfather was a Chiltern man. He was illegitimate, a fact no one seems to have been aware of until, on his deathbed, some legal matter required his full name. The poor old man was so ashamed; it had been the overshadowing secret of his life. His mother had married after his birth — not, I gather, his natural father. It was the same old story: she had been a servant

7

at a house, just a little grander than a farm, out Amersham way. My cousin Dick drove me past the gateway once, and said that, long ago, an old local resident had said to his father, "Ah, if your granma had played her cards right, that would have belonged to you now". Apparently this erring great-grandfather of ours never did marry, and having only unmarried sisters, I don't know what became of the property when he died.

My grandparents' marriage, which I estimate must have taken place in 1882 or 1883, was a physically active if not a happy one. Not counting the illegitimate Jack (who nevertheless did grow up as one of the family and took the name), there were nine children, born at roughly two-yearly intervals, my mother coming in the middle. Last came Ruby Dorothy, an afterthought and not too welcome; that was about 1902. Deeply resented by my eleven-year-old mother (for to her fell the task of looking after the younger ones), the baby soon became "our Doll", an engaging child who wriggled her way into Mum's heart and remained there for as long as they both lived.

There was another confinement after Doll, but a premature one — twins, who were born dead. Not in itself regarded as a tragedy, but Gran was in her forties by then, and her life was considered so endangered that the unheard-of happened — my grandfather summoned the doctor. Usually confinements were attended only by the old lady from down the lane. The children always knew when a new baby was on the way because there would be a bottle of gin in the cupboard, and when the birth was imminent the children would be sent down into the woods to play: "And don't come back till you're called". (It strikes me, in passing, that the old lady, with nothing to guide her but practical experience and folklore, made a better job of obstetrics than many doctors. Mum said she never heard of her losing a mother, and rarely a baby; and my grandmother appears never to have had a gynaecological problem in her life.)

Theirs was not a happy family. Grandfather ruled it with a rod of iron, and all were in awe of him. There may have been physical violence. On one occasion my grandmother, pregnant, walked out. She walked the two or three miles down to the station, where she asked the stationmaster to trust her for the price of a ticket to London — which he did — and took herself off to her sister's for as long as she thought it would take to "teach him a lesson". Apparently, in her absence he rallied and managed the running of the home and family surprisingly well, for a man who was very precise in his views on the rôles of the sexes. However, he shared the children's relief in seeing their mother return, and for some time afterwards was very subdued and considerate. But none of his children seem to have loved him, nor, even in later years, held him in any sort of tolerant affection which sometimes comes with time. But he was always kind to me, and had a dry sense of humour and a twinkle in his eye — but this was in old age when he had mellowed.

My grandmother not only brought up a large family with very little money and the most primitive of tools; she also served for a time as sub-postmistress and postwoman. Some days she would walk miles across the hills delivering mail, and every evening there was a sack of letters to be taken to the Halt for the evening train. All this, no matter what the weather or her state of health (and only in the upper classes were women allowed the luxury of feeling frail), and no matter that she was pregnant or recently confined two or three times during her stint — though presumably there would have been "maternity leave" during which the work would be covered by Grandfather and the older children. And all for a pittance, which nevertheless was the difference between "just managing" and living on the borders of starvation, for this was a time of great poverty in the countryside due to the slump in agriculture. At best, meat was a rare treat, though there was bacon at certain times when the family pig was killed; but the children usually got only the fat, which they were assured was the most beneficial to growing bodies; the lean bits had to be saved for Father. I don't know what bits the mother got, but in the way of mothers, I suspect it was very little of either. Strangely, living in the country as they did, they rarely had eggs in the house — though once in a while they might get a half for Sunday breakfast, as a treat. Milk was another rarity, except later, when the cow up at the Big House had calved and was producing more than the family could conveniently use.

At first my grandfather was gardener at the Vicarage, but then the parson died and he was out of work for a long time, so their only income was the little my grandmother could earn. There was no safety net then for situations like theirs, only charity which depended on the whim of the benefactors, and I'm sure my grandfather would sooner have seen his children die. Eventually he was taken on as gardener at the Big House on the hill — not really very "big" by the standards of the time, but the family owned much of the surrounding land and part of the hamlet beyond and were well-connected, the daughter being presented at Court at the appropriate time, with a town house to accommodate them in The Season. The head of the family was a Captain Musgrave (The Captaincy was in the local Yeomanry, and it is doubtful if he ever heard a shot fired, except in the shooting season). He was a benevolent despot who ruled his domain firmly but with dutiful concern. He was always ready with advice, financial, legal and moral; he adjudicated in disputes, and found employment for the younger members of his employees' families. In return, he expected those he employed and in whom he took patriachal interest to devote almost all their waking hours to the interests and service of the family. And, of course, to be members of the Established Church and vote Conservative — those who had the vote. This, he would have given them to understand, was for their own good; and no doubt he sincerely believed it. By the standards of his time, I suppose he could be called a good man.

My grandmother didn't find it as easy as Grandfather to "touch the forelock". He, after all, had been brought up within the still-feudal set-up of country life; she hadn't. However, she knew on which side her bread was buttered and so paid lip-service to the rules. Nevertheless, she didn't hesitate to speak her mind on occasion. Towards the end of the Great War, when so many aristocratic families were being wiped out by the death of their only sons, Mrs Musgrave (who, I may say, had only one son, either too young or too delicate to serve) expressed concern. To which my grandmother retorted, "Well, m'm, if ladies in high society had thought more about raising families and less about enjoying themselves and keeping their figures, they'd have plenty of sons to carry on." Mrs Musgrave gave my grandmother "an old-fashioned look". She herself had limited her family, according to Gran, by daily doses of Epsom salts. I don't know how Gran knew this (but then, the aristocracy would have been dismayed to learn how many of their most intimate secrets were common knowledge, and widely discussed below stairs).

My grandmother, as the mother of ten when her income would barely have kept one child in basic comfort, might well have tried the Epsom salts method herself; but she had funny ideas on the subject of family limitation. Years later she was heard to denounce Dr Marie Stopes as "a wicked woman". I can't think how she, who knew so much about family privation and was such a compassionate person, and something of a feminist, could disapprove of something so beneficial to womankind; but there, Gran was a patchwork of contradictions.

Although additions to the family were so frequent, and the process of birth itself can't have been too much of a mystery to the older children, my mother herself seems to have been woefully ignorant. Nothing was ever said to the girls to prepare them for what was to come. They were not even prepared for the manifestations of approaching womanhood, and when to their great alarm these appeared, my grandmother's chief concern seems to have been that they might tell the boys! I can't help feeling that, in the light of her own unfortunate experience, she might have been a bit more forthcoming. Surely she owed them that. As it turned out, her delicacy on the subject was to have disastrous results for my mother.

Poverty overshadowed everything. All the children were insured for a penny a week to cover funeral expenses if they died, and even this small amount was hard to find. Sometimes my grandmother would take them down into the woods to hide when the collector was due. Once he managed to grab my mother just as she was dashing off to join the others. He thrust his face down to hers and uttered terrible threats about what would happen if the money wasn't forthcoming. She was sick with terror; he became the great bogeyman of her young life.

As was the way with the country working-class in those days, the girls were sent out to service as soon as they were allowed to leave school. My mother left at thirteen — just before the leaving age was raised to fourteen. (My grandfather objected strongly to the new ruling, feeling that once a child could read, write and add up, it was its duty to relieve the family by earning its keep, a view shared by many.) My mother was kept at home at first, helping her mother. Then she went to stay in London with a childless aunt who had been ill with pleurisy (a condition my grandmother cured by long and vigorous pumelling with goose grease). Families were much more flexible in those days, and rallied round in times of sickness or misfortune. In large families, it wasn't unusual for at least one member to be "borrowed" from time to time by childless relatives, to their mutual advantage. My mother enjoyed her first glimpse of London — Edwardian now, colourful and exciting to a country girl.

Back home, once the little ones had reached school age, she was packed off to service. Her first job was at Thame Grammar School, where she burned her hand badly in the first week and had to leave. In due course she was sent off again, to a large, cold Rectory where she was the sole domestic, expected to fill every rôle, from cook/housemaid through to nursemaid, parlourmaid, and even, sometimes, church cleaner. There was never enough to eat, and she became ill — undernourished and overworked, no doubt. A short spell at home, then she was off again, this time to London, to one of those households where the mistress had social ambitions and very little money, with the result that again being expected to do the work of four or five grown women, she collapsed. This time there had to be quite a long period of convalescence at home, her mother fearing that she was going into a decline (which I suppose meant consumption — word too dread to utter).

There followed a period about which I know very little, and of which I write with sadness and a guilty feeling of betrayal. She became pregnant.

14

It is hard for us, at the end of the 20th century, to understand the shame and horror with which such an event was viewed. It was, of course, a common enough occurrence. In the country, the first birth often followed the marriage ceremony more closely than was quite proper. There were also families in which a little "love child" was accepted quite happily (and indeed, such children were sometimes particularly loved). But for parents like my mother's, who, poor though they were and carrying as they each did their own touch of stigma, still saw themselves as "respectable" (as indeed they were), the shame was more than they could bear.

As far as I can make out (and my mother told me nothing, ever) she had formed an attachment to a boy while working at the Rectory. He was the son of a small farmer, upright, hardworking, "godfearing" folk, who ruled their sons firmly and worked them hard. The attachment seems to have survived my mother's period in London and her ill health. With my grandfather's eagle eye and rod of iron, and her own working schedule, it's hard to see how this developed into an affair of some passion. That it did was, I'm sure, the result of my mother's naïveté, and her resulting condition must have been a shock so great that, indeed, she never fully recovered. It coloured one area of her life thereafter, and — indirectly — my sister's and my own. And, most certainly and sadly, my half-brother's.

There was no shotgun wedding. They were both under age, and obviously the boy's parents had no intention of sharing their son's services with a flighty young woman. And he doesn't seem to have been very concerned about my mother's plight. He ended up in the Grenadier Guards, and she seems to have been abandoned to her fate.

I suppose her father turned her out. She ended up in a Salvation Army home for unfortunate girls in Stepney, and there, in the hot summer of 1910 — the summer the Edwardian era died — she gave birth to a little boy. I can't bear to think of her frightened, friendless plight, and the setting; the hot, squalid street into which the two of them emerged to face the world, a world that must have seemed too drear and hopeless to be borne. But she was made of good, strong stuff, my mother. Somehow she made a life, of sorts, for herself. The little boy was placed with a foster family in Walthamstow, a very poor, hard-pressed family where he would often be hungry. It is as well that both he and my mother came from good country stock, which helped them in their battle for survival.

And then things took a turn for the better for Mum. She got a job with a family in Finchley, and she came to regard her time with them as the happiest of her in-service life — though, as ever, it was the usual grinding slog, with only one evening off a week and the occasional weekend. But the Simons treated their servants like human beings, even going so far as to confide in my mother about their family upsets, and taking her on outings and holidays. They were comfortable, middle-class folk who lived in a tranquil, secure world that must have looked as though it would last forever, shaken only occasionally by news items such as the sinking of the Titanic. (Mother was hanging out the washing and heard the newsboys shouting in the street. When she rushed indoors with the news, the mistress firmly told her it couldn't possibly be true.) The assassination of an Austrian Archduke in the July of 1914 didn't disturb them unduly. The following hot, heady days were quite unreal. And then, war, and "It will all be over by Christmas . . ."

It wasn't, of course, and in 1916, after a short sojourn in Cheshire with the family to escape the Zeppelins, Mum decided to respond to the Government's call for munition workers. It was a decision made with some misgivings. Low as domestic servants were on the social scale, they considered themselves far superior to "factory girls", who were said to swear and paint their faces and have loose morals. Mrs Simon was horrified when Mum announced her intention, and made it clear that her post would remain open if she reconsidered — and it was obvious she was sure Mother would reconsider before long. She didn't, but she remained fond of the family and kept in touch for some years, long after she was married.

A whole new world opened up for my mother. Hard and dangerous though the work was, her overriding feeling was one of freedom. Until she shed its bonds, she had never realised how feudal and claustrophobic the world of the domestic servant was. Even with an employer as good as the Simons, one was never "free"; one's life belonged to the Family. Security there was — as long as you abided by the rules — and protection from the cold realities of the world outside, but you paid for it.

The girls at the munitions factory were a different breed from any Mum had encountered before, London girls, reared in squalid streets, worldly-wise, with a rich vocabulary and incomprehensible jokes. It was they who considered themselves above domestic servants, and in quite a short time Mum came round to their point of view; it was the contempt and pity of the freedman for the slave. And the money was good; there was even a little to spend on fripperies, never before within reach, but she never forgot that the lean years would come again.

She seems to have been popular with her workmates, and she blossomed. She was friendly with a girl called Grace, a flirtatious, bubbly girl. Grace lived with a married sister, having lost both her parents. It wasn't a happy situation, because her brother-in-law made passes, she said.

This brother-in-law was at the factory gates one day in 1916. There was a young soldier with him. Grace shrieked with delight. It was her brother Ron, home on leave from the Front.

It was a momentous occasion for my mother, although she had no idea at the time of the impression she had made.

Ron said to his brother-in-law a bit later, "Who was that cracking girl with our Grace?" He had fallen in love, and I think there is very little doubt that, in his fashion, he loved her till he died.

My father was both a very simple and a complex man. He was intelligent in his way, which wasn't the way to be of much use to an ordinary working man.

That is, he didn't have a lot of common sense, and I don't think he can ever have been very good with his hands, even before the war deprived him of the proper use of one of them. Half of him was a dreamer and idealist, an incurable romantic. And he drank. Whether he would have done so had it not been for the war and its remembered horrors I don't know, but I suspect so, for life would inevitably have hurt him, one way or another. When sober and when the occasion demanded, he could impress with his firm and authoritative manner, and he was liked and respected by those who had only seen this side of him. But sobriety sometimes brought with it depression and self-doubt, and then only drink could sustain and reassure.

His parents had loved him dearly, that is certain. His father was born in Suffolk, possibly of Scottish extraction. He was trained as a cobbler, but was one of the roving kind, and at one stage was in Canada, hoping to make his fortune in the fur trade. He used to enthral my father with tales of his adventures, including the one where he was caught in a bear trap, and, alone, had to stitch up the wound with his cobbler's thread. He was a gifted raconteur, and the tale may well have been true, for this must have been in the 1870s, and anyone hobo-ing in the wilds of North America at that time could expect to have some pretty hair-raising adventures.

As far as I can gather, he came back from Canada on a whaler operating out of Dundee. In Dundee at that time, the young woman who was to become my paternal grandmother was growing up (was, indeed, grown up, having been born around 1857). Her family were respectably in trade, her maternal grandfather being listed among Dundee's prominent citizens in the 1820s. Her half-brothers kept a high-class bakery establishment (which, under another name, remains to this day). Her mother had recently died, and her father had married again. Somehow, she and my grandfather met and presumably fell in love. Her story of the affair made it sound romantic, and my father was happy to believe that. Anyway, they encountered some family opposition, and eloped. In fact, their marriage may well have been of the "unofficial" kind which was "illegal but valid" in Scotland until 1939, for I can find no official record of it.

They came south to London, to Kew and then Acton, where in the fullness of time their union was blessed — over generously, as were most Victorian families. There were six babies, three of each, but the two little boys born before my father died in infancy. It was a legal requirement then, and for decades after, for babies to be vaccinated against smallpox, which had been such a scourge. The two little boys reacted badly and died, with the consequence that, when my father was born, they didn't register his birth, hoping thus to avoid having him endangered. In fact he was vaccinated eventually, for there was a smallpox outbreak in the early 1900s, and his poor mother must have decided that this was the lesser risk. Happily, he suffered no ill effects. (He described to me how panicky people were at that time, passing money through bowls of disinfectant on shop counters, while people wore armbands to show that they had recently been "done", to avoid getting knocked.)

So, he was brought up as the cherished only son in a family of girls, very close to both his parents though they were probably not very close to each other. He often spoke to me with nostalgic pleasure of his Sunday morning walks with his father, just the two of them, along the Thames and out into the country, being sure to make it the minimum three miles which made them bona fide travellers, thus able to get served at a pub out of hours. The "old man" was an encyclopaedia of knowledge, country knowledge and a frontiersman's, with plenty of advice about life in general thrown in. One gem that has come down to me is: "Never get yourself tattooed, Sonny; it makes it too easy for the police to find you!"

Both parents called him Sonny. My grandmother became blind. "Always take care of your eyes, Sonny," she would say. Her blindness may have been something quite simple, which in these days — and perhaps even then — could have been cured if the money had been available. She used to feel his hair, which in those days was silky and red-gold; she hated him to have it cut. She was a clever and resourceful housewife, remembered long after her death for the spotlessness of her house and her washing. Of the latter, I remember an old neighbour of hers saying: "It was wonderful how she could actually feel where the dirt was . . ." My father used to help her to do the mangling. One day he mangled his forefinger and lost half of it. His mother couldn't see what was happening. (A thought occurs to

21

me: if it had been on his right hand instead of his left it might have been a blessing in disguise, for he might not have been able to join the Army, and the whole of his life — and ours — might have been different.)

Money was desperately short, so much so that my grandmother must have swallowed her pride and sent an appeal for help to her family. Her half-brother George came to the rescue, enlisting the help of a lady artist who lived along the river at Chiswick (I can't think how he knew her). My father would be sent to her house to collect a little packet, with strict instructions to give it to no one but his mother, and that no-one else was to know. Even with this occasional help, their plight was sometimes pitiful. My grandfather was not a wholly bad man, no worse than many husbands and fathers of his time, and in his good moods better than some. He was intelligent; he taught himself something about law, and advised poor people of the neighbourhood when they got into difficulties. He was a "personality", remembered as a small, bouncy, voluble man, very well-groomed with his little goatee beard.

His demon was drink. The money he earned at his shoemaking and mending had often disappeared over the pub counter before he got home, and Grandmother was at her wits' end to know how to fill the little empty bellies. Once she was so desperate that she sent her eldest daughter Lizzie out to pick flowers (Acton was more rural in those days), then the two of them stood outside various pubs, offering them for sale. I don't know if they sold any (my aunt couldn't remember) but they must have presented a pitiful picture, the blind woman and the little girl. One roisterer who did take pity on them was none other than my grandfather who, in the dim light and in his befuddled state, didn't recognise them. He became quite misty-eyed and maudlin, and pressed a shilling into Lizzie's hand — a whole shilling! It was a story my aunt told with relish.

Lizzie had a grudging affection for her father, although he didn't have a lot of time for daughters. As a little girl she remembered being put on the table to entertain his cronies when they came in from the pub. He would throw down two crossed knives and make her do the sword dance. She was small and lithe and bright as a button, fond of music and dancing all her life, so she didn't object, and I think in his way the "old man" was proud of her. She was so like him in so many ways but without his considerable intelligence. No doubt he considered "education" wasted on girls, and she went through life barely able to read or write.

Lizzie married at nineteen a local young man who had a good job in the sword factory. It was neither a very happy nor unhappy marriage. They had seven children, plus a "non-starter" who, coming too late in life to be convenient, met a premature end by means of a hot bath and a great deal of gin. Of Liz's sisters, May went into service and Grace into the nearest factory. Both parents were dead by then.

So my father became an orphan, and changed from being a cherished son to a tiresome younger brother whose existence was a bit of an irritation. However, he had an earning potential now, so was tolerated. He had been a plumber's apprentice, but either because apprentices didn't earn very much or because he was proving to be not very good at it (both, I suspect) he left and took a job in the sword factory with his brother-in-law.

The war came. One day he went out with his swimming things wrapped in a towel, not saying a word about his real intention, and came back home an enlisted soldier.

He joined with his friend Ginger, who must have been under age, for the Recruiting Sergeant said, "Go and have a walk round, sonny, and see if you can come back a bit older." It was all a great lark, though for my father it was much more than that. He was going to fight for his country, and would have echoed Rupert Brooke's words about 'thanking God for matching him with the hour', if he had known them.

His anecdotes about the war, and life and death in the trenches, were such a familiar background to our lives in later years that my sister and I were early inured to the horror. I wish now that I had listened more attentively, but had we done so our lives might have been even more overshadowed than they were. Even as it was, the shadow of war was always hanging over us, a khaki-coloured cloud, blood-streaked and ominous, and I was certainly no more than five years old when I first thought: What if there's another war and Mummy and Daddy and Mary are killed? (Strange that I thought I myself was immortal.)

But I can't remember in any sort of detail what he told us. He would break off sometimes, his eyes watery and glazed, the memories he had conjured up suddenly becoming too much for him. "You don't understand!" That was when he'd had a drink. Ordinarily he didn't talk much about it. I do remember, though, his telling us that when he and his mates were behind the lines, foraging for something to make a fire during one of the periodic lulls, they came upon an old windmill, and started chopping up some of the wood from it. The local mayor came up in a state of great agitation, complaining because the mill was reputedly the one from which Edward the Third of England had watched the Battle of Crécy at which the Black Prince had won his spurs. It is refreshing to know that between the bouts of unspeakable barbarity there were still people to care about these things.

He came home on leave in 1916, perhaps before the Battle of the Somme, which was to haunt him forever, and on that leave, he went to meet his sister Grace from work, and fell head over heels in love.

For the rest of his life, he looked back upon that leave as its high point. His family had welcomed him with open arms; welcomed, too, an excuse for a round of parties to end all parties. He managed to persuade my mother to come to one these — on a Sunday! She went, though with grave misgivings, and melted in the face of their expansive hospitality. The rest of the leave was spent in hedonistic gaiety, including visits to the theatre to see such improving entertainments as "A Little Bit of Fluff", in the company of sister Grace for propriety's sake — but before the ten days' leave was up, Grace was no longer considered necessary.

It was all over too soon. My mother didn't accompany him to Waterloo; I think his sisters did that. His feelings may be imagined. Deeply in love, he was too unsure of himself to have proposed (he seems to have had very little experience of girls, in the romantic sense, though surrounded by them at home). His letters to my mother are casual and jokey, not love letters at all, really, yet beneath the banter his feelings reveal themselves. He writes in happy anticipation of his next leave and of the end of the war. No doubt he touched wood as he wrote.

He managed to survive the inferno of Trones Wood, though the experience seared him for life. But later, during some close encounter with the enemy, he got a bayonet through his right forearm. Ironically, the resulting paralysis might have been considered some sort of blessing, but at the same time he sustained a blow which knocked him out, and he woke up to find himself a prisoner.

At home, he was reported missing, believed killed. Nothing else was heard of him for over a year.

My mother must have been saddened, but she had learned not to get too fond of young men on leave from the Front. She had had her own Waterloo mornings, seeing off returning soldiers. She had four brothers in France, one of whom, poor little Bert, had been killed in 1915 after only a fortnight at the Front. The other three had all had their brushes with death. She once described graphically what it was like, saying goodbye to them on the station platform. She remembered the sea of khaki and the bleak, glazed faces, the memory of which made her want to cry when she described them fifty years later. The few brave smiles nailed to the mast, the weeping women, straining for one last glimpse, clutching through carriage windows for the last touch of beloved fingers, as the long, slow train pulled out. Then the sense of desolation, the muffled sobbing, and the dispersing back into the grey streets. I see London in those days as endlessly grey, endlessly November.

To lose an admirer was nothing new to my mother. At least two had preceded my father. How serious these friendships were I don't know, but she kept their photos for the rest of her life. She never spoke of them. As to her feelings for my father, she admitted once, with a twinkle in her eye, that at the beginning she didn't think him anything special. Life went on. It was a series of highs and lows. Death was always somewhere around. Few days passed without someone in her circle losing a dear one or hearing that they had been maimed. Workmates would wear black armbands, and for a little while would stand apart from the camaraderie of factory life, their mourning respected. Distraught mothers would appear at the factory gates, and someone would disappear from the assembly line. The murmur would go round: "She's just heard her brother's been killed . . ."

And then one day early in 1918, my mother received notice from the Swedish Red Cross that my father was a prisoner of war. A printed card followed, sent by him, crossed out as appropriate:

"I am/am not in good health" and "I have/have not received any mail". But the date was that of a year earlier, so it was impossible to tell what the current situation was. Then there was a proper letter, and an address to which she could write (the seriousness of his feelings for her may be judged by his contacting her rather than his sisters). She must have written back, because in his next letter he is back to something of his old form: ". . . They say that if the war doesn't end, we shall be repatriated when we're forty-five, so only another twenty-two years to go . . ."

For him, thinking of her had been like the light at the end of a long, dark tunnel. In the early days of his captivity, he had been treated very badly, being sent to a punishment camp (for being cheeky, I think). There had been weeks of solitary confinement with long stretches with neither food nor water — a deprivation he could never forget. "Hunger is nothing," he would say, "but thirst — oh my God!" But in the last few months, things got better, and he even made friends with his captors, both sides agreeing that war was ridiculous.

By then, it must have seemed to both sides that the dreadfulness would never end; war was a way of life. Then suddenly it was over, not with a bang, but with a whimper.

As far as I can make out, no-one told them — they just found that they could walk out of their captivity. And they did. Alone, for what must have seemed good reasons, my father just set out to walk in what he judged to be the general direction of home. People along the way — the ordinary people of a starving and defeated Germany — must have given him enough food to keep him going. Just enough. He crossed the border into Holland somewhere near Nijmegen and collapsed at the gate of a convent. The nuns took him in and treated him with great kindness until the Red Cross arrived and took him home, a shattered old man of twenty-three. He always had a soft spot in his heart for nuns after that.

In England, the news that an Armistice had been declared was received at first with incredulity. My mother said that when the maroons sounded, at eleven o'clock, people at first just stared at each other. Then, as the news ran round, tools were dropped on benches and factory gates were flung open and they streamed out, merging with the workers from all the other factories and laundries. Every factory hooter was going at full blast, people everywhere were laughing and hugging and kissing, and they piled into buses and any other available vehicle and swooped off to the West End to join a swelling throng of rejoicers there. My mother's most vivid memory of the day was of being lifted up on to one of the lions in Trafalgar Square by a large Australian, wearing his hat. (Anyone knowing my mother in later years would find this hard to imagine, but a lot of people were doing untypical things that day.)

Some weeks later, my father proposed to her in hospital. She hesitated. She had by this time become fond of him, but she had seen him during the brief spell of leave he had been allowed, when his return had been celebrated by his family in their usual style. Already, drink was a problem; he had so much to forget. But he wore her down. I think she thought she could save him from himself, and in a way she was right — but no one could have saved him totally. He promised to give up spirits and kept his promise most of the time, though he found other ways of blotting out the past when things got too much for him.

And so they were married, at eleven o'clock on a November day, almost exactly a year after the Armistice, and it was after that that they came to live in the country, for my father's health.

It was the start of a partnership, loving if not always happy, of not quite forty years.

CHAPTER
TWO

Early Voices

There was nothing picturesque about our hamlet. It was a collection of perhaps a dozen houses set bleakly amid cornfields. There was a row of Victorian brick cottages and an unbeautiful pub of the same vintage, a pair of semi-detached villas and, in a side lane, two houses of slightly grander proportions but no architectural pretensions. Then there was the factory, and our bungalow (if it can be dignified by such a name) and then, farther down the lane where the scenery improved, there was a farm owned by a bad-tempered Scot called Willie Logan, who seemed to live in a perpetual state of war with the rest of the inhabitants, including my father who was usually well-disposed towards Scotsmen. And on the other side of the little river (at this point a deceptively innocent-looking ford) lived the gamekeeper, Walt Collier (whose children were our playmates), in the only picturesque dwelling in the area, white-walled with a backdrop of woods owned by the mysterious squire, as invisible and omnipotent as God.

We didn't have a fence in front of our garden; we had a platform, like that of a country railway station. It had been used for loading munitions on to Army lorries during the late war. I was ashamed to live in a house which had a platform where everyone else had a fence. But it was fun to play on. I remember a summer evening when my sister Mary and her friend Alice France did the Charleston on it. The Charleston must have been very new at that time, and perhaps the France family was new to the village, bringing with it ideas from the big world outside. Mary's dancing wasn't very good — even I could see that — but Alice was an expert. I can see now the flashing feet and flailing arms. She could only have been about eight, and one wonders where, in those pre-television days, she got her expertise.

Another unusual feature left over from the war was the little railway — but that only skirted our garden and we weren't allowed to play on it. There was a miniature track, overgrown now, and a line of little rusty trucks which had once carried explosives out of the factory yard across the field, over the river, up the slope to the woods where there were mysterious little huts where, I believe, various dangerous substances had been tested (a sylvan setting for a rehearsal for slaughter). I suppose the war had been the hamlet's heyday and some of the inhabitants may be forgiven for mourning its passing, especially in later years when the Depression had closed the factory and reduced it to silent dereliction.

My parents seem to have been fairly happy in their Army hut — but perhaps that is in retrospect. The period of transition can't have been easy for either of them. Both, in their different ways, had one foot in the past, my father unable to shake off the war (part of him didn't want to) and my mother adjusting herself to married life after several years as her own woman. One of her reasons for marrying may have been to provide a home for her little boy (nine at the time of her marriage, which he attended). It is possible that part of her affection for my father was her recognition of him as a kind man, not too conventional, fond of children, and able to take Harry's existence into his stride (not easy for a highly moral man such as my father was).

Harry loved and was loved by his foster parents, and within the limits imposed by their grinding poverty they had been good to him. He, along with their own children, knew real hardship, and the surroundings in which they were brought up must have been soul-destroying in their dreariness. The war had brought its sorrows. The family's three sons had been killed, one in dubious circumstances after he had been forced to return to the Front after a spell of hospital leave during which it was obvious he was suffering from a nervous breakdown. (My brother and one of the grandsons were taken to the seaside — their one and only childhood outing — on the insurance money resulting from one of these deaths; it rained all day and they spent the whole time under the pier.) From all I have heard, Harry's foster mother was a good woman, though, worn out by her worries and sorrows, she indulged in a little weakness: she drank Dr Collis Browne's Chlorodyne. I remember seeing advertisements for this popular elixir, but can't remember them saying anything about curing worries and sorrows,

though curing everything else, but apparently it did —
for a little while. She used to send my brother down to
the chemist's to buy it for her. It cost one-and-
ninepence, and on her meagre income that took a lot of
finding. But, as Harry said, "Poor old girl, she had to
have something."

To be transferred from this background into the
heart of the country could only be an improvement,
one might think. It didn't work. Harry never really
settled. Once the novelty had worn off he was homesick
for the squalid streets and the friends and family he had
come to regard as his own. I think he tried again from
time to time in the next few years, but he never took to
country life. I think, too, he found it hard to come to
terms with my father's drinking, hating it when Dad's
behaviour gave rise to jeering comments from the other
children — something my sister and I had later to take
in our stride. (Harry's foster father wasn't a drinking
man.) Harry led the hamlet boys astray with his
London ways (or so the locals said; no doubt it was
fifty-fifty). As he grew into his teens, the escapades got
wilder. There was a brush with Willie Logan over some
misdemeanour with an air gun, and some talk of a
letter-box being set on fire, but whether he was actually
involved is uncertain. In a narrow community the
outsider is always the scapegoat, and if the outsider is a
"townee" he's a natural target. He was intelligent, and
he was bored. If he could have got some sort of further
education, his gifts, such as they were, might have been
harnessed and he might have developed into a fine
young man; but there was no question of that. On his

last period of residence with us he got a job at the biscuit factory in Ware, but that didn't last long. At eighteen he joined the Army ("for three square meals a day," he later said), and after that we only saw him once, briefly, until he was quite grown up.

My father, too, suffered a little from being an "outsider" in the claustrophobic hamlet community — but he didn't see it as suffering. He saw himself as a cut above the ordinary country working man, and it didn't grieve him in the least that they never really came to look upon him as "one of themselves".

My mother was more readily accepted, being a country woman and knowing country ways, but she never quite became "one of them", and was never quite at home in Hertfordshire. She was liked and respected, I'm sure, in every place we lived in, but was always a little apart, and even at that tender age I felt that in some way my parents were superior to the parents of my friends. The feeling never left me.

The pub loomed large in my father's life as ever, and presumably he had drinking cronies. My mother met other young wives at "Women's Afternoons" organised by the local gentry. I don't know how frequent these were, and only remember one, held in someone's barn, at which there were a great many very noisy children, and the tea was very hot and dark and the cakes very good. Also I think there was, at regular intervals, a mother-and-baby clinic in the next village. This must have been a new idea, one of the few good things to come out of the Great War — the reason behind it being, presumably, that the country needed strong young men to replace the millions lost in the recent slaughter; otherwise, who would fight the country's future battles? And you couldn't start too soon.

There was, of course, very little to do in the evenings, apart from the pub which was very much the men's domain. The factory bosses, perhaps unusually for those days, did make some attempt to provide a little bit of social life. They ran Whist Drives, in an upstairs room, and on those occasions my mother, who didn't enjoy cards, was put in charge of the gramophone. My father loved to relate how, on one such evening, Mum made a mistake. Almost every public occasion in those days ended with the playing of the National Anthem. Everyone stood to attention; it was almost a sacred ritual. This time, my mother inadvertently picked up the wrong record, something quite unsuitable, and instead of the anticipated "God Save the King", the patriotic audience was treated to something like: "Yes, We Have No Bananas". My mother was mortified, and my father never let her forget the incident (I'm sure it was because he was just a little in awe of her that he loved it when she did something "silly").

Such friends as my parents had tended to be "outsiders" like themselves. There was a very pleasant family called the Woodfords, who later moved back to the North London suburb from whence they came, and the Yorks, who were obviously our social superiors, for he was a school teacher — not locally; he "commuted" (though that wasn't a word one came across for many years). These friends most unusually had cars, and I remember our family being taken by the Yorks one

Saturday afternoon, in about 1928, to Bishop's Stortford to see Charlie Chaplin in *The Gold Rush*. It was my first visit to the cinema, and the film was, of course, silent and seen through a flickering haze of silver rain. The darkness of the auditorium and the goings-on on the screen were too much for my fragile nerves: I screamed. I had a very penetrating scream, which had in its time brought neighbours running. Once started, I couldn't be stopped. My father, who had been enjoying the film, was obliged to take me out (thus wasting his ninepenny ticket) and had to keep me amused in the car park until the others joined us at the film's conclusion, rubbing salt into the wound by describing how hilarious it had been. The Woodfords, too, took us out on one occasion when the hood of the car blew off. I remember the shock of being transported from the cosy security of the car's dark recesses to sudden exposure to light and wind and weather. "Uncle" Woodford soon repaired the damage with a bit of string and we were on our way again.

Both these families were, apparently, atheists. Not aggressively so, and I don't think there was much discussion of the fact, but it was an unusual thing to admit to in "ordinary" circles. My mother must have found their views rather shocking. I remember her saying to me, when I was quite small, that "Uncle" and "Aunt" Woodford didn't believe in God, and they believed that when you died, "that was the finish". It seems a strange sort of conversation to have with a small child, but no doubt a question of mine had prompted it. I was a great questioner, and much given to thinking up awkward subjects to discomfort my mother.

The hamlet had no church or chapel, but we went to Sunday School. This was run on Presbyterian lines by the aunt of one of the factory bosses, a lady with missionary leanings and an aggressive taste in hats. We gathered in the upper room which was used for the Whist Drives, and we sang the usual hymns, about the friend for little children above the bright blue sky, and Jesus bidding us shine. And I remember Harvest Thanksgiving, with red apples on the windowsills and the westering sun slanting in. The room always smelled of apples, and of damp hymn books.

The hymns my mother sang to me (and I say "me" rather than "us" because I was the one whose hair had to be brushed hard and disentangled every evening — it was that sort of hair) were robust and unAnglican. I sat on Mum's lap, and the singing was supposed to help me forget the pain. She sang: "Hold the Fort for I am Coming", "Shall We Gather at the River?" and others from Sankey and Moody's rousing collection. When my protests became particularly loud, she brushed all the harder and sang louder:

> Oh, if I had wings of an-gels
> I from earth to heav'n would fly,
> And I'd reach the gates of Zion
> Far beyond the starry sky.

The hymns I learned thus at her knee I relearned at my father's in soldier's bitter parody. But he never swore, and never much overstepped the boundaries of good taste. In the places where doubtful words occurred he sang "Marmalade and jam" — which I also sang, believing them to be the real words. Once, years later, when someone expressed surprise that I knew a certain very unladylike song, I was acutely embarrassed, realising that I had been singing this apparently innocent ballad for years, unaware that it was in fact very rude indeed.

Songs played a large part in my childhood. My father loved to sing and had come from a family where music was important. I say "music" and make no apologies for using the word — for why should popular music be denied that description? It gave them, and him, great pleasure, and he had an enormous repertoire: music hall ditties, love songs, comic songs, a snatch or two of Gilbert and Sullivan, Edwardian ballads (which he sang very soulfully — though sometimes tongue in cheek) — even the occasional few bars of opera which he could only hum or whistle (not even knowing they were opera). But what he liked best was Ragtime, which had its heyday just before, and during, the Great War. He knew them all, and my sister and I could join in most of them: "Way Down on the Levee", "Ragtime Cowboy Joe", "Everybody's Doing It", "Ragtime Violin", "Alexander's Ragtime Band" — most long forgotten now.

A great pleasure to Mary and me in those early days and during our growing years was the visits of our London relations. They would explode noisily onto the scene, bringing with them excitement and gaiety and an atmosphere of urban sophistication. They were not, in fact, in the least sophisticated; they were perhaps rather simple, with a childlike enjoyment of the passing moment. In their cheerfully fashionable finery, unsuitable high-heeled shoes and exotic scent, I thought my aunts and older female cousins very beautiful, and longed to be like them (though I wouldn't have wanted my mother to be like that; she was beautiful as she was, and smelled wonderful). I don't know what our bucolic neighbours thought of the invasion, when the open charabanc came bumping down the dusty country lanes, its passengers swamping with song the silence normally broken only by skylarks. I suspect they took it as further evidence that we were an alien breed. I loved the excitement, and enjoyed being fussed over, particularly by my cousin May's young man, Fred, who had "patent leather" hair which I smoothed stickily as he carried me for miles on his shoulders.

May and Fred were frequent summer visitors, coming on Fred's motorbike. The other family members usually came on Bank Holidays (there were no paid holidays as a right, I think, until about 1938). August Bank Holiday was the high point of the year, the first weekend in August at that time and for long after. After that, the grown-ups had nothing but the drab long nothingness till Christmas.

When our visitors came, they went to the pub which must have profited considerably from the influx. There, and back at the house afterwards, they sang. Uncle Phil always brought his melodeon, and he would play all the latest songs, "My Blue Heaven", "Bye Bye Blackbird", "All By Yourself in the Moonlight", "Ramona", and the pretty romantic Irving Berlin ballads like "You Forgot to Remember".

But although they liked to get a bit sentimental once in a while, mostly our guests liked something a bit more cheerful and robust, particularly the older songs, including some very slightly naughty ones (but never downright bawdy; my mother would never have stood for that). Obviously, my memories of their repertoire at that time are unreliable, but I remember snatches — I could always pick up songs quickly — and the rest I learned over the years, for the basic programme remained the same, for as long as their sing-songs lasted, which was as long as the older members of the family lived. "Has Anybody Here Seen Kelly?" they sang and "K-k-k-Katey" and "When Father Papered the Parlour". The songs just poured out of them, and they knew every word, including the verses which preceded the "refrain" — all songs seemed to have some sort of prologue. Then there were the solos, several members of the family having "their own" song, and woe betide anyone else who tried to sing it. I remember my cousin Ivy's song was, predictably, "Just Like the Ivy on the Old Garden Wall". She had a sweet, frail voice, and loud shouts of "Quiet!" and "Order!" would almost drown the opening bars; joining in was frowned upon until the second chorus. My father's favourites, which he sang with tremendous verve, were, of course, the Ragtimes. But he also sang an Army song to the tune of "Dixie", which made me cringe with

41

embarrassment because of its reference to "making tea in a biscuit tin someone washed his trousers in", which seemed to me very rude. And when towards the end of the session the beer was taking effect and things were getting a bit maudlin, he would sing, very dolefully, "Trumpeter, What Are You Sounding Now?" — and there would be an awkward silence after this, an embarrassed reluctance to return to the spirit of revelry. In fact, if it was resumed, it had to be worked up to gradually. It would have been considered bad taste to follow "Trumpeter" with, for instance, Aunt Liz's speciality, which was a ditty called "Izzy Azzy Woz" with its gem of a last line:

> I've called to ask is Izzy worse
> Or izzy azzy woz?

This, and others in a similar vein, were accompanied by a curious little bobbing motion, in which my father joined. Their mannerisms, the lift of their shoulders, were almost identical, no doubt an echo of their late father's. Aunt Liz was very plump at one stage, which at a height of under five feet made her look like a little barrel, but in later years, because she hardly ever ate properly, she became thin and wizened before her time. But she had plenty of bounce, and could be very charming, quite unselfconsciously. She was wryly humorous, warm-hearted and the object of much real affection. But she had a temper, her daughters said, and could have an acid tongue, though I never experienced it.

Sometimes during the school holidays her two youngest children, Nellie and Ronnie, came to stay on their own, and they were the cousins we knew best throughout our childhood. They were lively and streetwise, and Nellie wore beautiful dresses because her aunt on her father's side, who had lost her own children, was a dressmaker and loved to make Nellie look pretty, which wasn't difficult because she was little and doll-like. It was on one of their early visits that her brother enlightened me on an aspect of life which had been puzzling me. He greeted me as I emerged from the (outside) lavatory with the news that, "the cat has laid some kittens!" All was suddenly clear. My mother's insistence that kittens came from heaven was all wrong! Perhaps she didn't know herself? Kittens were laid like eggs! And I knew about eggs, because my little friend Dottie, the gamekeeper's daughter, told me. The chicken's tummy opens and out pops the egg! So that was the great mystery! (I honestly didn't connect human birth with this process, then or for many years afterwards, and it was several years after that I got it right.) I should add that in the matter of the kittens, their stay with us was very brief; they "went back to heaven" very quickly, so I reflected that it was hardly worth their coming. I obviously had a lot to learn about life.

I was a difficult child. It had not always been so. According to my mother, I was sunny-natured till I was two, when I caught a particularly virulent form of measles, and in its aftermath developed pneumonia, which was probably the number one killer of young children in those days. My life was despaired of. It reached the stage where the flicker was barely discernible. My poor mother, bending over my cot, cried, "Oh Ron! She's gone!" But he, hardly daring to look, said, "No, look, she's still breathing . . ." and it was at that point that the fever passed its peak — helped, Mum always insisted (and who are we to argue?) by prayer and camphorated oil. When the doctor called next day, prepared to find me dead, he found me on my feet, trotting around, exhibiting my famous stamina. He thought my recovery a miracle. But something had happened to me, and I was never the same again.

The convulsions started after that. When those subsided, I started throwing tantrums instead. So notorious were these that if we were going to visit relations, our hosts would gird themselves and await my arrival like Rome awaiting the invasion of the Goths. My mother didn't let me off lightly: I'm told she was driven to thumping me with the copper stick, and shutting me in the cupboard — a therapy not likely to be recommended nowadays for the treatment of an unstable child, but the phrase "highly strung" wasn't in a mother's vocabulary in those days, and if child psychologists existed they kept a very low profile. It was still thought by many worthy parents that to spare the rod was to spoil the child. Neighbours and aunts and even my sweet little Granny advised Mum to give me "a jolly good hiding" (incomprehensible phrase), and still I raged and screamed. "I was at my wits' end," my mother admitted later. No physical punishment made the slightest difference. Her advisors confessed themselves baffled, deciding that some children were so inherently naughty that nothing would cure them. What they didn't understand was that when I was having one of these tantrums pain meant nothing to me; I even inflicted it on myself at times. There was nothing for it but to let me exhaust myself. After which, I was usually unwell and at the receiving end of my mother's loving concern, my naughtiness forgiven and forgotten.

Through all this, I accepted as a matter of course the support of my loving sister. It was only later that it struck me as exceptional for one so young to be so patient and concerned for such an exasperating sibling who was hogging all the attention. Poor Mary, she had few reasons to love me. By the standards of the day, she was considered plain, I was considered "pretty" for my hair was blonde and curly, hers straight and brown. Apparently, one of the hamlet women had said, peering into my pram, "Oh, she's prettier than you are, Mary". I think that thoughtless (and totally untrue) remark haunted her for the rest of her short life, but, bless her, she never let it show. With all this "goodness", she was by no means docile. She had a taste for adventure, and I remember her being at the forefront of many an expedition, at least one of which had the village parents scouring the countryside for us; she was no more than seven at the time. She was, and remained, intensely interested in life — she cared much more for it than I did. My main concern at this time was to see that I got as big a slice of the cake as possible. I was a horrid child.

I liked Saturdays. There was an air of freedom about them, even to us pre-school children. Not like Sundays, which apparently it was naughty to enjoy too much (though the rules were waived when our pagan relations came down; they actually sang songs on Sundays, but there seemed to be a tacit agreement with the Lord that those Sundays didn't count). Saturday was Daddy Saucepan's day, which taught me how important money was, otherwise we would never have known the pleasures and pains of making a purchase as we almost never saw a shop, our groceries being delivered by a man with a pony and trap from the nearest village. But Daddy Saucepan sold sweets, and he came on Saturdays. He came in a rattling, dilapidated cart pulled by a tired old horse who had to keep stopping to crop grass to keep his strength up. Daddy Saucepan dealt in many things; he sold paraffin and doormats, and kettles and saucepans and white enamel pails. The tinware hung suspended from the back of the cart and rattled so loudly as it bumped along that you could hear it half a mile away. I recall a Saturday morning in summer — nearly midday, for the sun was high — and we were playing in the spinney between the factory and the hamlet proper. We had a little house, and had some broken cups and plates and a good deal of interesting household rubbish, for we were playing with the Bardoes, who were experts in the collection of interesting jetsam. But the older children were getting bored, and one of them shinned up a tree. From there he could see right up the lane. The familiar clanking and jangling came faintly from the distance.

"He's coming!" The boy slid down and we all dispersed, Mary and I to find our Mum, who was whitening the step.

"Can we have a ha'penny, Mummy? Daddy Saucepan's coming!"

My mother grumbled a bit and made some protest, and said something, too, about our playing with the Bardoes, of whom she disapproved. I suppose two little pairs of pleading eyes broke down her resistance, and she got up from her knees and fetched her purse and gave us each a ha'penny. We raced back triumphantly to where Daddy Saucepan waited. He exchanged our ha'pennies for two marshmallow alligators. He was a silent, ragged man with string round his waist, and his filthy, paraffin-moist hands tainted everything he touched. We ran to show Mother our purchases. She was obviously uneasy but couldn't bring herself to forbid us to eat when we were so happy. I recall the taste of that alligator now as I write, nearly seventy years on. It was delicious — paraffin and all.

The Bardoes of whom my mother disapproved were a poor, sprawling, exuberant family who lived near the pub. I suppose that was my introduction to snobbery: all men were born equal, but the Bardoes of this life were even less equal than we were, and if we played with them we might Catch Something. Strange that my beloved mother, the kindest of women, and coming from a large and poor family herself, should have taken that attitude. That there was a difference between the Bardoes' poverty and that of her own family is arguable. Mrs Bardoe wasn't an enthusiast for housework, but then, neither was my maternal grandmother — nor Mum herself, though she tried, endlessly. It was generally accepted in the hamlet that Mrs Bardoe Wasn't Clean. This, in the eyes of the respectable working-class, was a worse sin than immorality, no allowance being made for the fact that there was probably nothing in poor Mrs Bardoe's upbringing or domestic situation to encourage her to be a housewifely paragon, raising as she did something like seven children and seeming to be almost permanently pregnant or post-natal, while trying to satisfy all those country appetites on one man's wage (if he had a wage). The phrase I heard often throughout my childhood was, "Soap and water's cheap enough." Nothing is cheap enough if there is no money coming into the house.

I liked playing with the Bardoe children, and I liked Mrs Bardoe. She was plump and cheerful (what I saw as plumpness was probably pregnancy or nursing motherhood). The phrase "earth mother" comes to me now, for that is the image I have. I only remember her clearly from one occasion, but it is a sharp picture, filed away in the mind's archives. I had been playing with the children in their backyard. It came on to rain, and Mrs Bardoe told us to come indoors. I see clearly to this day that bare room — actually quite bare of furniture, without so much as a bit of worn lino or rag mat on the floor. But there was a good fire, and we sat on the hard boards in front of it, and Mrs Bardoe made us pancakes (perhaps it was Pancake Day). I know now that her generosity in including me in the feast probably deprived her of her own share. The pancakes were thick and fatty and we ate them with our unwashed hands, dripping grease onto our clothes — and they were the best pancakes I have ever tasted. I was annoyed when a knock came at the door and I heard my mother's voice asking if I was there. I see Mrs Bardoe now, flushed and beaming cheerfully, explaining that we had been enjoying ourselves — as indeed we had.

My mother didn't exactly cluck, but I had the impression of being gathered swiftly under her wing and we scurried home. I don't remember being prompted to thank Mrs Bardoe for her hospitality, though no doubt I was. I expect I was scolded, because I remember smarting under the injustice of it. Perhaps I had earned Mum's displeasure by not telling her I was going; surely it wasn't just because it was the Bardoes? But sitting smugly on our rag mat in front of our gleaming stove, surrounded by all the comforts of home, I couldn't help reflecting that it was nice to live where I did, with pretty curtains and pictures on the walls, and to be my mother's cherished "baby" instead of one of a large brood.

I only vaguely understood her objections. I knew that everything she did, she did for us, Mary and me, therefore there was some reason why the Bardoes were Bad. Now, a long time mother and grandmother myself, I can't judge her harshly. It may be that there was some epidemic going the rounds, and I was considered particularly vulnerable during my growing years. I had been at death's door; it was important that I avoided infection. Infection was the constant dread of mothers. Routine childish ailments could and did kill, and there was no protection, apart from the smallpox vaccination. And anyway, her concern wasn't one-sided. When Mary and I had measles, it was a matter of pride to Mum that no one else in the hamlet caught it.

We didn't often go away, except on the occasional charabanc outing which my father got up through the pub — for example, to the Empire Exhibition at Wembley, of which I have no memory. At least one Christmas we spent in London; it was one of the few snowy Christmasses of my childhood and enchanted me. But although such contacts with the outside world were rare (not as rare for us, who had outside connections, as for many in the hamlet who had been born and bred there), we were not completely insulated. I do just remember my father's "cat's whisker" wireless set, on which, he insisted, he once "got America". I find this hard to believe. He was hopeless at things technical — though having read a good many books he could sound quite impressive when he spoke of them. I don't know if he put his little crystal set together himself, but if he did, then it's even more unlikely that he got transatlantic messages; I'd be surprised if he got the next village. But of course, we believed the American story throughout our childhood (as did he) and we thought him very clever.

His politics at this time were solidly Conservative; indeed, he used to say that he thought he would be the last Conservative left on earth. With his wartime disillusion, it seems incredible that "King and Country" still made him swell with pride. His pride in the Empire was enormous (and this would still have been true of perhaps nine people out of ten in those days). I don't, of course, remember the General Strike, but I know he was sworn in as a Special Constable and was issued with a whistle in preparation for the Revolution, if and when it came, and he was firmly on the side of Law and Order. He used to get invitations to go to Police Sports Days and Conservative events. Mary and I went to Conservative children's parties at Christmas (where the food was very good and all the "nice" children went). All of which was at odds with his outlook in later years. As for my mother, she had suffered too much in the feudal atmosphere of her childhood to be a wholehearted upholder of the Conservative ideals. But I suppose the great red bogeyman of the Russian Revolution, so recent in memory, frightened a lot of ordinary people. "Better the devil you know . . ." And no doubt those who had influence in high places saw to it that that outlook was maintained for as long as possible.

But a change was coming.

I was four-and-a-half when I left my native hamlet, in the late spring of 1929, and for one whose infant memories were so strong, it's strange that I recall so little of our going.

It must have been a fairly traumatic event, a decision taken hastily, as far as I can judge. There were changes being made at the factory. The old bosses were gone, the Depression was beginning to loom, and I think it was at this time that much of the work was being moved to a factory in the town.

It looks as though my father may have fallen out with the new regime at the hamlet branch. There had already been a clash of personalities, and he may have resigned on the spur of the moment, becoming jobless and homeless on one high-handed impulse.

My mother's feelings may be imagined. There were no welfare organisations then for the feckless and/or unfortunate; he had given up his job so there would presumably be no dole money. It must have seemed to Mum that disaster was staring us in the face. She always put on a good front and treated my father as head of the house, supporting him in his decisions, but I think she would have allowed herself a tightening of the lips on this occasion, and that could be formidable indeed.

Her parents came to the rescue (Grandfather must have undergone a softening of the heart in the years since her earlier predicament). We were offered a temporary home with them while my father stayed behind in Hertfordshire to look for a job and a home for us. I presume the furniture was put into store. He got taken on at the town factory, which must have demanded some swallowing of pride. He went into lodgings, all too conveniently in a pub, where the landlord and his sister made him very comfortable — perhaps too comfortable.

My grandparents were living at that time at The Hollows, a tumbledown thatched cottage in the Chilterns. Picturesque it certainly was, for it actually had roses round the door with a roof that sprouted grass and walls that grew moss. It was barely habitable, but a tall, ugly brick building had been added, comprising a sitting-room and bedroom approached by a dark and treacherous stair. In addition, there was a lean-to extension of corrugated tin, and this was divided into two small bedrooms which were to accommodate my mother, Mary and me. There was a big garden, and an orchard behind a hedge, running down to the beechwoods which stretched all the way along the top of the hills to Stokenchurch and beyond. Also in the garden was an overgrown pond, a large vegetable patch which supplied the family's needs for most of the year, some flower beds, a chicken run, and a well — a tank, actually, so that the water we drank and used for all purposes was really the drainings off the fields, water being scarce in that part of the Chilterns. During one or two hot summers when the source of supply dried up my grandfather had to pay for a tankful to be horse-drawn from Stokenchurch, at thirty shillings a load (a week's wages). Needless to say, any baths we had at that time were infrequent and very shallow.

Mary was a great favourite of Granny's; I, for some unaccountable reason, of our grandfather's. But I was always a bit in awe of him, and was always being warned not to sit in his chair, nor to make a noise in case I disturbed him, and not to touch anything that was his. But I still hung around him, and tweaked his moustache sometimes, and said things that made his eyes twinkle. I treated him warily most of the time,

aware of his reputation as an ogre. I didn't love him; I
don't think anyone did; but I did have a glimmer of
affection. I think he recognised in me a bit of himself;
we were both cantankerous, and if I could be said at
that age to have a sense of humour, it was perhaps of
the same caustic brand as his own.

He was still working at that time for Mrs Musgrave,
who lived alone now, apart from one elderly servant, at
a smallish Victorian house just up the lane. Grampy
had a curious relationship with her, each respecting the
other while taking delight in spiteful little digs, and
behind her back he made fun of her cruelly. She was
tall, spare, aquiline of feature, every inch an Edwardian
grande dame. Most clearly I remember the band of
black ribbon she wore round her scraggy throat, usually
adorned with a cameo brooch, and her high autocratic
voice (in common with most of her age and class, she
had a special voice for addressing the lower orders,
higher and louder than for her peers). In a way, she and
my grandfather were two of a kind, in age, even in
physical type, and they were both wilful, supremely
selfish, redeemed only by a strong sense of noblesse
oblige on her part and a sense of humour — albeit a
waspish one — on his. And they shared a love of cats.
Mrs Musgrave's cat was called Adolphus. He was large,
fluffy, overfed and spoilt. Though he was a "cat" person
himself, Grampy couldn't resist the temptation to get
his own back on the old lady through her beloved cat,
who in turn treated Grampy with lordly contempt.
Most days there was a tale to tell of Adolphus's doings,
his being upset or pleased: "Adolphus was highly

delighted," Grampy would report, and sometimes "That didn't suit milord, you may depend." I used to swing on the gate, looking up the lane for Grampy to emerge from behind the Close hedge, watching him limp towards me, leaning on his stick; he liked that.

Apart from her constant worry that we might upset Grampy, Granny was delighted to have us under her roof. She was such a dear and loved company and was always bustling and cheerful, taking a lively interest in everything we did. She was a gregarious soul, and living without close neighbours she must often have been lonely once most of her family had fled the nest. She loved a little outing; perhaps it was her Cockney roots. She belonged to the Mothers' Union down in the village — not, one would think, a den of iniquity, but my grandfather didn't approve of her going to the meetings. She went, nonetheless, and put up with his grumpiness when she got home.

Somehow she managed to get herself included in a trip to the Flanders battlefields. I think she was probably present at the unveiling of the monument at Delville Wood, for I have a snapshot of it, but this must have been as a part of a wider tour, for this area doesn't seem to have been one in which her soldier sons were involved. I should add here that, during the war, when my Uncle Bill had been too badly wounded to be moved, Captain Musgrave had paid for my grandparents to visit him in France. He recovered, physically at least, and now was employed at one of the vast cemeteries there — and, incidentally, had in 1921 been part of the escort of the Unknown Warrior. Probably the later tour in which my grandmother took part was arranged by the Mothers' Union, and she qualified as a bereaved mother. So she had been "abroad" twice — no mean achievement in those days when many ordinary people lived out their lives without crossing the borders of their native county.

The Hollows, as its name implies, lay between two gentle slopes beside a dusty lane lined with holly trees. Beyond this lane, opposite the cottage, had been more beechwoods so that the house had been enclosed by woods on two sides, but not long before we joined the household there had been a big fire, and it had swept through the trees, seriously threatening the thatched roof, for one spark was all that would have been needed, and the wind was strong. My grandmother, who had a sensible, matter-of-fact relationship with God, said her prayers, and, as with my own mother on the day of my birth, the wind changed just as the fire reached the lane. But the beautiful woods on that side were gone, and in its place was a nightmare landscape of black ash and gaunt white tree stumps, through which we could still pick our way, getting our shoes full of ash and our socks filthy. Now, Nature was healing the scars.

The soil must have been very rich and the brambles that struggled through soon flourished and bore luscious blackberries and raspberries. The former we not only gathered for pies and preserves, but also (we children, and Mum and Aunt Doll) for a dye factory. It was a messy business, and slow and uncomfortable, what with the prickles and the fallen logs and ashes, but

I think the going rate was ten pence a sack, and that wasn't to be sneezed at. The lorry used to come round and collect the fruit of our labours, by which time hands and clothes were dyed a rich burgundy; rather gory we must have looked, with the old battered lorry resembling a revolutionary tumbril. It seemed a pity to me to sacrifice the fruits of the earth so bounteously bestowed on the altar of fashion; but there was still plenty left for eating — until the 26th October, that is; it was a well-known fact that the Devil put his foot on them on that date and eating them after that would do you no good at all. Incredible as it now seems, my mother and her family seemed earnestly to believe this, as did most of their country contemporaries. And no new moon appeared without my mother and grandmother going out to look for it for fear of being caught out and seeing it through glass, this ritual being accompanied by a turning over of the household purse. Later, my mother pretended she did it in a self-mocking way, but the truth is she wasn't taking any chances.

We at The Hollows, along with both households of Musgraves, the Websters at the farm, and a family in the gamekeeper's cottage, didn't consider that we belonged to the hamlet, and our address was "The Hill" — considered (by us, at least) quite superior. In the hamlet proper there was a collection of flint cottages, surrounding an almost mediaeval yard, and a little tin chapel, a pub (very basic) and two or three of the "better" type of houses occupied by "upper middles". I suppose the total population, both parts, was forty at the most. I have a photo, taken at the annual garden party given by the Musgrave son and his Italian wife for their retainers and families, and for most of the rest of the hamlet because it didn't seem kind to leave them out. Mary and I are in the front row, the "squire" is presiding in an attitude of benevolence, his wife wielding a guitar (which I don't recall her playing) and to this day I recognise and could name at least half the rest. Including Mrs Turney, in her brown felt hat.

Mrs Turney was always there, though I wonder how she found time to stand still long enough to have her photo taken. She was always on her way somewhere, with quick, purposeful strides, sometimes accompanied by a rustling sound as though she wore a taffeta petticoat — which seems unlikely, unless she had found one somewhere. There was a raw, rustic wholesomeness about her — which had nothing at all to do with cleanliness, though her rosy face shone as though it was well scrubbed with carbolic soap. She always wore the same felt hat, wide-brimmed and firmly anchored, from which fell dark loops of hair (which might have been quite beautiful, only we never saw the rest of it). She wore a long, neutral-coloured skirt which reached the top of her (man's) boots; this was usually covered by a sack apron, the pocket of which bulged with her lunch (that is, her mid-morning snack), for she worked out of doors when the work was available: haymaking, hoeing, harvesting, and if none of these was in season she went stone-picking. Mindless drudgery that was, out in all weathers, bent over the grudging chalky fields, wearing the skin off blistered fingers. A job like that was beneath the dignity of all but the really hard pressed. But Mrs T. was always cheerful, and always busy and breathless. She loved to talk, but seemed to have no time for it, for her conversation (monologue, rather) always took place on the hoof, so to speak. She came towards you and started talking, and continued as she passed, only a second's pause being allowed when she was beside you, then she was off again, talking as she drew away, raising her voice as necessary as the distance between you lengthened.

Mrs Turney was a source of quiet amusement to my grandfather. Her husband Will was little and wizened and always seemed depressed. They never seemed to communicate, though presumably they had had their moments, for there was a son, a gangling youth known inevitably as Turniptop. Mrs T. was disapproved of by the hamlet males because she had scant respect for that holy of holies, the taproom of the local pub, where she could, and did, take her ale like a man. Will took no notice of these intrusions, sitting in his corner looking gloomily at his hand of dominoes. Only once, my grandfather reported, he was stirred to take an interest. Perhaps it was Christmas; anyway, in a celebratory moment Dan'l North forgot himself so far as to put his arm round Mrs Turney's waist (it was news to me that Mrs Turney had a waist). Will, from his corner and his one pint, broke his habitual silence by protesting, in tones of thunder and a face the colour of an overripe plum: "Dan'l, Dan'l, thass my property!" (pronounced "prarperrty"); so perhaps there was more to the relationship than met the eye. One likes to think so.

A great pleasure to Gran in the last active decade of her life was her nightly toddle up the lane to the pub for her glass of beer, taken in the lamplit back kitchen, for only hardy souls like Mrs Turney cared to beard the lions in the taproom, and the chilly parlour was rarely opened, and never in the winter. (Needless to say, Grampy disapproved of these outings, but in her old age Gran was perhaps past caring.) In later years, when we came to stay at The Hollows in the school holidays, Mary and I used to accompany her on her nightly jaunt, and share a bottle of bright red Kola, sitting on wooden stools in the pub kitchen and listening to the local gossip, most of it a dull catalogue of people's ailments and misdoings — not much in Gran's line, I think; in any case, she only heard about a quarter of what was said, and clucked a bit in what she thought were the right places. But she had a knack of hearing when the conversation took a turn for the gynaecological or scandalous, and could make it clear with unfinished sentences and pursed lips that such things were not suitable subjects for her granddaughters' ears.

Afterwards, on the walk home, she would give us a lecture on the stars, which we looked up to between the banks and high hedges that concentrated our view to a narrow, glittering strip, beautifully visible in the dark landscape. The lane was very dark indeed, narrow and heavily pitted. I shall never know how Granny never had a fall, not so much because of the effects of her glass of beer, but because she always looked at the stars and not at her feet. Perhaps she got her priorities right.

When I look now at the country-weekend cottages in the estate agents' windows and read of the rustic delights on offer, I think back to The Hollows and its sagging thatch and bare laths where the centuries-old plaster had fallen away, and I wonder how it was that it seemed to us so cosy and delightful and utterly safe. Safe it was not, for in a year or two it was to be condemned as unfit for habitation, and at the time we lived there, only the kitchen was considered suitable for use. This had a floor of uneven brick, and an enormous fireplace all but filled one wall. Beside this was a bread oven, no longer in use, which projected outside and had a domed roof. It had no mod. cons. of course. There was a big scrubbed table on which food was prepared (and where I scratched my letters). There was an enamel bowl for washing up and a zinc bath for washing clothes and bodies. On a stool in a corner stood a pail containing the water we used for drinking.

Every drop, of course, had to be hauled up from the well. There was no pulley, no winding handle; it was just a matter of flinging down the bucket on the end of a rope and heaving it up. Mostly this was done by my mother, though Aunt Doll took a turn, frail though she was, after she rejoined the family following a spell in hospital (where she had recovered, miraculously, it was considered, from meningitis). Granny, at around seventy, did it when there was no one else available. I don't think Grampy would have dreamed of helping except in the most unusual circumstances. The wonder

61

to me is that large families had been commonplace in the country; presumably they would have been even larger had it not been for the heaving and hauling many women had to do during their pregnancies.

But presumably the man of the house performed the even more disagreeable task of emptying the lavatory buckets. I never at any time saw this happen, at The Hollows or elsewhere, so it must have been a task performed under cover of darkness which must have made it a chancy business. The contents were disposed of in such a manner that what came out of the garden went back into it; nothing was wasted. The idea doesn't appeal to me now, but we thought it the most natural thing in the world then, and the produce from those cottage gardens was the most luscious and prolific one could wish for, with never a chemical coming near them.

The lavatory itself (referred to rather charmingly as the dunniken, a word peculiar to Oxfordshire and its neighbours, I think) was part of the cottage, not a separate building more hygienically placed. It was entered round the side, where the sunflowers and yellow roses grew (my own garden). Inside, it was really quite pleasant and comfortable, with spotlessly whitewashed walls, and usually smelling of nothing worse than Jeyes' Fluid, except in prolonged hot weather. And it was decorated by a gallery of coloured pictures from a supplement to the *Auckland News*. These were supplied by the lady for whom my grandmother did a bit of cleaning. She had a daughter in New Zealand and had recently visited that country herself, her visit coinciding with a dreadful earthquake which I heard my mother and grandmother discussing with much concern. But for me, New Zealand was a sunlit country full of blue-eyed girls and lambs and rosy apples (which I was to know well in later years).

Many happy half-hours I spent in the dunniken in tranquil contemplation, and many a tale I wove as I sat there, tales in which I figured as the beautiful heroine to whom incredibly glamorous things happened.

In my old snapshot album there are two little photos of Mary and me, sitting bolt upright in our grandparents' garden, looking distinctly sour. These were taken by Mr Lambert. Poor old man, he lived alone in a tiny house by the church, and eked out a meagre income by taking photos professionally. Heaven knows how he managed in such a sparsely populated area; I can only assume he had a pension. He was always immaculately dressed, hatted, of course, and with a high wing collar on the hottest day. He rode a tricycle, with his antiquated equipment strapped on behind. Fussy and pathetically anxious to please, he came to The Hollows one afternoon at my mother's request to take our photos, to send to our father, but by the time he had got us suitably seated and had dithered around with his camera and tripod, and considered angles and light and all the other things, we were bored and irritable, and the cats we were photogenically nursing escaped. Mine was recaptured and is being gripped with grim determination. (I think he was called Billy; Gran always had at least one cat called Billy, irrespective of sex.) Poor Mr Lambert, he tried so hard, and the results were so disagreeable that I doubt if Mum bought many. But I remember the occasion so well, I in my best dress with my long green necklace (which I later swallowed, with interesting results), Mary sternly upright, obedient to instruction but too bored to smile.

That photo is, for me, the last of babyhood, for when we left my grandmother's we left an era behind. From then on I was no longer a baby, to be alternately indulged and scolded but not taken too seriously. I was five years old, big enough to be thrust into a waiting world. I didn't look forward to it, and had a sneaking feeling that my all-powerful mother would find some way of keeping me closely safe with her forever.

I was to be sadly disillusioned.

CHAPTER
THREE

Green People

We returned to Hertfordshire from our sojourn in the Chilterns in the early spring of 1930, when I was four months past my fifth birthday. My father had found us a little house — a very little house, quite new, one of a pair on the edge of a green, rented from a disagreeable old man called Smith (a Plymouth Brother, and no great advertisement for his faith) who lived nearby.

We had seen little of my father during the past months, and I was shy. We walked up from the village in the rain, I clinging to my mother, longing to be back in my grandparents' cosy, crumbling cottage.

My father had done his best to give us a warm homecoming, though his choice of decor wasn't to my taste. But our furniture was there, remembered now, including the gramophone and the red and blue glass vase which I had thought so pretty, as well as the picture of Weston-Super-Mare and his framed letter from the King, the German helmet and pair of Mills bombs, standing on the mantelpiece where other people would have had china dogs. It all began to come back to me.

There wasn't much to explore. Although new, it had few mod. cons., but it did have an indoor sink and tap which we had never had before. And (joy of joys!) it had an indoor lavatory, with a chain to pull. I was up and down stairs a dozen times in the first hour, trying out this marvel, insisting that I needed to. There was actually a bath, too — but no hot water, so bath night was as tiring for my mother as it had always been — more so, for she had to light a fire under the copper in the scullery, heat the water, and carry it upstairs, bucket by bucket, so our baths were no deeper than they had been at The Hollows. But the novelty never palled.

The Green was just that, a stretch of grass, not very big, with a little country road running across it, down to where it crossed the bourne by our house. Ranged around the green was a sprinkling of cottages and small brick villas, perhaps late Victorian, and on the south side, some way back from the road, was a small Jacobean former farmhouse, in which lived the odious Mr Smith and his browbeaten wife. This would later play a part in our own lives (not to mention one day housing a world-famous artist). The pub stood just round the corner, kept by Tom Petty and his wife. Mrs Petty was to become the nearest thing to a friend my mother had on the Green; she was gentle and intelligent, not much like a pub landlady. But then, the pub was a simple alehouse, its trade limited for most of the year to the frugally-spending locals.

Tom was the Council roadman, for it wasn't expected that a small country pub would wholly support the tenants. There was almost no daytime trade, except at weekends. The Green bore fewer signs of poverty and burgeoning population than most hamlets in those days. Its inhabitants kept themselves to themselves much more than is usual in such a community. Almost all the residents were middle-aged, or behaved as though they were; and most shared the same surname. And, most unusually, children were rare. There was one little girl across the green with very respectable parents, and I struck up a friendship of sorts with her; but she was obsessed with keeping her socks clean. Then there was a widow with one son, about my sister's age and known for some reason as Yodel. He wasn't too bright, but was the apple of his mother's eye. She was a vigorous countrywoman with a passionate interest in her neighbours' doings and vociferously on the defensive if she thought they were taking an interest in hers. She kept her handkerchief up her knicker-leg.

And then, next door to us, there were the Browns. Or the Edwardses. Or Cochranes. We were never sure what to call them. My mother politely called the lady of the house Mrs Brown because the man of the house was called Mr Brown. And the youngest child, Dolly, was called Brown sometimes and Edwards sometimes, but it seems to have been accepted that she was Mr Brown's child. She was two years old and had tight white curls. Mrs Brown had tight black curls and looked like a gypsy, and she had a fiery temperament and a rich vocabulary. Mr Brown had hardly any voice at all. He was a sad, pale man with a drooping moustache. He had been a traction engine driver, going round the farms, but was now said to be dying of consumption. He hardly ever went out, but sat by the window and liked to watch the children playing. It's hard to imagine how such a mésalliance as the Browns ever came into being.

The other members of the family were definitely Edwardses. When they were not Cochranes. Sammy and Gracie were about ten and eight; they were nice children and didn't get themselves into trouble. Sammy could get a bit boisterous at times, as boys will. He would sometimes come flying out of the back door with his mother in hot pursuit, threatening to belt his bloody arse which shocked and interested me. I thought he would be terribly worried by this threat, but he would go off laughing (when well out of reach) and his mother would recover immediately and smile at me and say "Hullo, dear" — as though nothing had happened. In my sheltered life this was the first time I had come up against real swearing, but I had no difficulty in recognising it, and knew better than to go indoors and repeat it to my mother. The only time I had used language of which she disapproved was once when I said: "Oh Gawd!" — an expression picked up from a girl down the lane. I felt much aggrieved by the vehemence of my mother's scolding. When I reflected what I might have said, I felt righteously hard done-by.

I don't know how people like the Browns managed for money. There were other, grown-up, children. One, Jem Cochrane, rode a racing bike and had a job. He was cheerful, and presumably generous to his mother, for they never seemed to want for anything, and their lifestyle was certainly no worse than ours. There were also two grown-up girls living away, perhaps in service. One came to stay with her mother after a spell in hospital. I can only guess the nature of her ailment from the fact that my mother spoke to her in the tone she reserved for the bereaved or those suffering from a gynaecological disorder — though in the latter case I can only speak with hindsight. Mary and I envied the Edwards children their grown-up, glamorous sisters. They were so pretty, and wore beautiful earrings.

Another family came to live briefly on the green in the less attractive of the thatched cottages. There were three little girls, but we didn't play much with them. The only thing I remember about them is that they rarely wore shoes or socks. More shockingly, they revealed that they hardly ever wore knickers. I suppose this was in the interests of economy. They themselves thought nothing of it, and were hugely entertained by my shock and disgust. I didn't dare tell my mother. The word "knickers" was hardly ever uttered in our house; "drawers" was permitted; bottoms were referred to as "B.T.M.s".

But before we made ourselves acquainted with the neighbours — indeed, before my mother had finished putting the house to rights — I had a shock of another kind.

Mary had started attending the village school nearly three miles away. My mother decided that my enrolment could wait until after Easter when the weather would have warmed up. For me, the thought was shelved. Something would crop up so that it could be postponed again, I was sure. I would cling to Mummy and no one would be able to prise me away and they'd give up and go.

A knock came at the door, and there stood the dread figure of the Attendance Officer.

My mother went into a long explanation about my belated registering. Well, yes, she knew I should have started after Christmas, only . . . etc. etc. I hung behind her, glaring as balefully as I could. Gradually, the truth began to dawn: she wasn't winning! There was a power even greater than the power of mothers! I was going to have to go! I couldn't believe it. She was going to let them take me! When the dreadful man had gone, I pulled out all the stops, shrieks, breast-beatings, the whole grand performance. It was no good.

So exhausted was I that when the next day came I was drained of all feeling, except conscious of a dreadful hollow where my heart used to be, as I trudged down the long road to the village with my mother, my cheese sandwiches and two handkerchiefs clutched in my sweaty little paw. I had no tears left to shed when she disappeared from view, leaving me in the Infants' playground.

The little girls were all quite nice to me on that first morning, for being the lone new arrival, it amused them to "mother" me. One of them gave me a daffodil to give to the teacher. I can see it now in a jam jar on Miss Woodrow's harmonium, and smell the distinctive classroom smell, a mixture of disinfectant, chalk dust and unwashed boy. Miss Woodrow was the usual maiden lady of uncertain age (I doubt if she was more than thirty-five at the time). She gave no indication of either approving or disapproving of me. She was scrupulously fair, though I didn't think so at the time, because I was never chosen to fill in the "weather" squares on the wall chart (a different colour for each day). And I never did get to use the coloured chalks on my little blackboard; these were reserved for children who showed artistic promise, which I patently did not. Perhaps she thought I was too pushy.

At midday we ate our sandwiches in the cloakroom, sitting on narrow benches up against the coats and clothes pegs. Later, on wet days, it was to prove a miserable place to sit, especially when the radiators were on and the wet clothes steamed and made our backs damp. But the first day was all right, and the novelty of having washbasins with running water interested me, so I kept washing with the raw red carbolic soap until my hands were sore. The lavatories were across the yard, and the toilet paper consisted of cut-up squares of a publication called (I think) the *Teachers' World*. Once, much later, I had occasion to interrupt a teacher at her lunch, and found her at her lunchtime task of cutting up the paper and threading it with string. (I should like to say, here and now, that the *Teachers' World* was not ideal for the purpose.)

From the first day I was aware of the social distinctions. Children are dreadful snobs, and it dawned on me quite early that Mary and I fell between two stools. In village schools there was (interestingly, the situation is probably now reversed) a gulf between the actual villagers and the children who came from outlying hamlets. In those days the latter were easily identified by their dusty shoes and unbrushed teeth, and the fact that their lunch (at mid-morning playtime) usually consisted of bread and jam while the village children had proper biscuits, sometimes even with iced animals on them, which I desired above all things.

The little circle into which I was accepted on my first morning was made up of villagers, with clean fingernails and carefully pronounced aitches and Ovaltiney badges. The children with whom I journeyed to and from school came almost entirely from the other side of the tracks, socially speaking. With few exceptions, I think it has to be said that they were not enthusiastic absorbers of knowledge, though native cunning they had in plenty, and if Human Biology had been in the curriculum they would have left the rest of us standing. (I learned the facts of life in my first week at school and didn't believe them for more than ten years.) Mary and I spent our school lives feeling that we were neither fish nor fowl, a little outside both categories and never quite accepted by either — but I think Mary adapted more easily than I, and was always popular.

Up to the age of seven, the hamlet children were transported to school by Mr Prior's coal lorry, so it would have been pointless for us to be dressed too immaculately, even if our mothers could have managed it. The smell clung, too, which further separated us from our village classmates. We sat on rickety forms on each side of the lorry, and there was much squabbling and shoving for the two coveted places by the open end. We slithered a bit going downhill in the mornings, making physical contact closer than one would have wished. Sometimes we — or more usually, they — burst into song; not nice little children's songs, of course (anyone attempting those would be greeted with derision) but something like:

> There's a good time comin' but it's ever so far
>   away,
> That's what I sez to meself, sez I, Jolly good luck,
>   Hooray!

which I suppose was the top of the pops, so to speak, at that time. But that, of course, was on the homeward journey. There was no such lightness of spirits on the morning ride.

There was a good deal of rudery from the boys (we had no supervision, Mr Prior being out of sight and earshot in his cab). In those early days I don't remember being teased too much. I kept my mouth pretty well shut, as they didn't care for my accent (or lack of it). One or two of the girls were quite nice to me; Florrie Fowler was one and Eva Shipton another. Both came from big Council house families, the Fowlers having the edge, just, when it came to intelligence. Her brother Georgie was about my age, small and dark and cheeky, but not as bad as Billie Wicks. The Wickses looked as though they had gypsy blood and Billie must have grown up quite handsome. I was aware of him because he delighted in shocking me

— and goodness knows, he must have recognised in me a tailormade victim.

Then there were the Tadgells, Stanley and Doris. Socially, they just about made it to the bottom rung, even by hamlet standards. They were the middle two children in a large, undernourished family which were to be our neighbours when, later, we moved up to the Tye, and Doris was to be my Best Friend for a time. I don't suppose they ever knew what a full stomach felt like, but I remember clearly a moment of triumph they had. It sometimes — rarely — happened that someone had something left over from their lunch bag, usually a curled-up sandwich, certainly nothing to make the mouth water. However, there was an occasion when, presumably to mark some red-letter day, the Tadgell children each had a piece of chocolate Swiss roll. Cake of any kind must have been a rare event in that household; shop cake was unbelievable. Yet there it was. Not only that; the slices were enormous. And there, triumphant, Stanley and Doris sat. Somehow they had both managed to get through the day without consuming their treat. No doubt by some prior agreement, they had hugged their secret to their breasts all day, longing for the moment of revelation to come, savouring the anticipation. Now they ate, with exasperating slowness, unrolling the dark sponge and licking off the cream with caressing tongues as the rest of us watched enviously (for few of us were in the shop cake class). I don't suppose anything in life ever succeeded those moments of pure happiness for Stanley and Doris.

74

I neither liked nor disliked school. In the very early days I must have decided that I disliked it — which, I gathered from my hamlet-based classmates, was entirely natural; liking it would have made me a real oddball. So when Lizzie Wicks explained to me one day that we didn't have to go, I was all ears. The Wickses and I and a couple of other children waited for the coal lorry at the crossroads by the little church, in the limbo between the Green and the Tye. Lizzie explained that all we had to do was hide in the churchyard until the lorry had gone. I felt rather doubtful, but allowed myself to be persuaded that it was a great lark and would be the Open Sesame to membership of The Gang. I was disturbed to find that only the Wickses, Dolly Hunt and I could see what a lark it was. The others went on waiting for the lorry. From behind the church we watched it arrive, saw Mr Prior lift them on board, and then it was gone, and we were on our own in a world grown suddenly very quiet and cold, and strangely uncomfortable. We emerged warily from our hiding place and discussed, somewhat half-heartedly, what games we should play. I doubt if five minutes had passed before the truth began to dawn on me: freedom was an illusion! I longed for nothing more than the comforting bondage of life's rule book. I simply wasn't one of nature's rebels.

Someone was coming. Lizzie dragged us behind a hedge. With mingled horror and relief, I realised it was my mother, with Mrs Hunt I think, walking to the village. Lizzie hung on to me, but I broke away.

"Mummy, Mummy! I haven't gone to school!"

I don't think we were scolded; not at that stage. We had the long walk to the village, in silence.

My mother had a word with the teacher, who directed us to our places without reproach; her stern look and chilly tones were enough, as were the later jeers of our classmates. I never transgressed again.

Looking back, I suppose I was a reasonably bright child, by the standards of village schools in those days. And the standards were, at least in the basics, quite high, higher than in the post-Second War years. Learning was drudgery, and no-one pretended otherwise; the chanting of tables rings in my ears as I write (interesting that old methods are currently coming back into favour, after decades in the wilderness). The idea that children might enjoy learning was just beginning to be considered; my parents thought my Infant class was wonderful, comparing it with the gloomy austerity of their own. The three Rs were paramount. The only pupil I knew who couldn't read and write after the age of seven was poor Bob Ankers, a shambling, educationally sub-normal lad who was always treated with kindness and patient encouragement, and probably ended his school life rather better qualified than if he had been in the care of some educational psychologist.

Reading was a piece of cake to me because I had already gone through the early stages at home. I fumed with impatience as I had to chant with the rest: "Jack is on the sack. Pat him on his back."

I remember the illustrations. The books were of frayed linen, and the pictures portrayed well-bred

76

children with nannies (the latter in starched aprons and frilled caps with lace streamers) all living in some golden Edwardian summer. Before long I had gone through all the books on offer, after which I used to be packed off to the corner of the classroom with the slow readers, to listen to them struggle. I could never understand why the effort brought beads of perspiration to their brows. I don't know that my impatience endeared me to the hamlet children (from whom, needless to say, my "class" was mainly drawn). I enjoyed writing — enjoyed most subjects, really, except sums, with which I could just about cope. I wasn't keen on handicrafts, but managed to learn simple sewing and made my mother spend a precious sixpence on a bib that I had "embroidered" with a squirrel — which I insisted on wearing for my meals for at least a week. "Art" I had no flair for, though I did try, and got some pleasure from it. Singing I enjoyed. Our teacher had a wheezy old harmonium on which she picked out tunes with one finger and, as it was out of tune anyway, we always sang flat. My memory's ear conjures up the sound now:

> When Father takes his spade to dig,
> Then robin comes along,
> He sits upon a little twig
> And sings a little song.

The last flatly rising note still grates, in recollection. They were happy years, the two we spent at The Green the first time round, once the shock of school had been overcome. The pattern of the seasons was beginning to colour my life and add to its richness. I enjoyed something about each of them, though January and February brought their trials, usually in the form of colds and chilblains, to both of which I was to be martyr for most of my life, whereas Mary seemed virtually immune. But even the winter months had their compensations. November, being my birthday month, was always exciting. I have always loved autumn, and the nip in the air and the scent of bonfires stirred me — and stirs me still — with sharp anticipation and delight. I loved the cosiness of murky afternoons when I arrived home to my mother's welcome and the glow of coals inside the murmuring grate. It was my special time, when I had my mother to myself, for Mary, being older and not having the blessing of transport from school, arrived home an hour after me, only just making it before dark in midwinter. My mother was not only practising economy in not lighting the oil lamp until it was too dark to see across the room; she loved the gloaming, and hated drawing the curtains while any daylight remained, as I do still. I remember particularly a winter's day when I must have come home feeling a bit unwell. I remember sitting by the fire when I came in, the blackened kettle singing gently on the hob for our cup of tea, and I was cuddling our purring tabby cat while Mum set out the cups, and it seemed to me that all the love and warmth and comfort in the world were wrapped around me.

Spring, of course, was good — or would be, we felt, when the bitter winds had stopped blowing. We drew snowdrops on our little blackboards at school, and there was frog's spawn in the brook which I ran through my fingers with sensuous pleasure, followed by the tickle of tadpoles, and finally by the tiny, jewel-like frogs which hopped like grasshoppers from the palms of our hands.

Easter marked the beginning of the visitors' season, though that didn't get under way properly till Whitsun, which from then on became my very favourite time. The combination of fine weather and burgeoning nature, with the cuckoo calling from dawn to dusk from the bluebell woods, the horse chestnuts in bloom, and the green speckled with daisies — it was almost too much. I sometimes felt my heart would burst with the wonder of it all.

> . . . Thou hast no sorrow in thy song,
> No winter in thy year . . .

I knew what that meant before I learned the poem; it summed up my feeling that God was indeed in his heaven and all right with the world, and the dark, bleak days were gone forever.

And the visitors: I loved the excitement, and the difference the lively household made, with nice things to eat, no constant preoccupation with what was good for our bodies and/or our souls. And laughter, and loud voices, and songs: the old remembered ones, plus current favourites like "Springtime in the Rockies", "Happy Days Are Here Again", and "We're Happy When We're Hiking" — this last because it had suddenly become fashionable to be healthy and people poured out of the towns in shorts and open-necked shirts, punishing themselves with unfamiliar exercise, on foot or bicycle: ". . . ten, twenty, thirty, forty, fifty miles a day".

They used to come striding earnestly, swinging their walking sticks, down the road across the green, stopping to sit at the wooden tables in the pub yard and drink their draught bitter, dutifully filling their lungs with our good country air (while deploring, sometimes, our good country smells). The cycling clubs, burgeoning now, were more working-class and were younger, livelier, and they chattered more and called out to each other and giggled and teased the girls, who all seemed to have crimped fair hair and be called Reen.

I should add that our own London relations took no part in this new-fangled enthusiasm for good health. "The country" for them was sitting outside the pub rather than inside. They told each other repeatedly how much good it was doing them. Sometimes my father jollied them into taking a walk in the fields. He would lead them in straggling and protesting procession ("All who's barmy, follow me," was his exhortation on one occasion). The ladies were never equipped for this sort of exercise; they were accustomed to teetering along pavements in their high heels, and in the country they tripped over tree roots and lost their shoes in the mud, and couldn't negotiate the stiles because their skirts were too tight (or, later, too long) and they sometimes had to be carried over ditches; and they squealed in the

80

long grass for fear of creepy-crawlies. All of which made a good tale to tell over the evening pints, to the great delight of the local old boys.

While the grown-ups were over at the pub in the evenings, we children were allowed to get ourselves supper and get to bed when the spirit moved us. Incredibly my mother went along with this, not even insisting that we say our prayers on these occasions, heightening our sense of unreality. Mary and our cousin Nellie, who was nearly twelve and quite grown-up despite her tiny stature, would cut us slabs of bread and cheese, and sometimes fetch us crisps from the pub — real tuppenny bags of "proper" crisps (not the broken ones which were a penny and were the sort we usually had on the very rare occasions when we had them at all). We would then lark about for a while before putting ourselves to bed on the boxroom floor, five or six of us, fitting onto the mattress "tops to tails", and we would sing, and giggle, and tell stories until we fell asleep. I was always the first to go, which annoyed me because I fancied the others had the best of the fun while I was unconscious.

These visits from her in-laws were a great safety-valve for my mother. Although they made a lot of work in that inconvenient little house, all the women gave a hand (men, of course, did not, at least not on the domestic side, nor were they expected to). And they always brought food with them — more than enough, for all the wives worked throughout their married lives and were never really short of money as we were. Acton was one of the areas with a tradition of working wives, because of the many laundries there (its nickname was "Soapsud Island"). Presumably there was time off for child bearing, and perhaps the early stages of rearing, but then the extended family would be roped in, this being before the availability of crèches. Otherwise, I don't remember any of them, male or female, being out of work. They worked hard and played hard, and if they ever took life seriously, it never showed while they were with us. So, for a couple of days here and there throughout the summer Mum was able to convince herself that life was good, not the penny-pinching struggle that it really was. And, most important, she could stop worrying about my father's drinking, for these were his own people, who loved and accepted him for what he was, and thought nothing of the times when he was Not Himself; after all, some of them were Not Themselves for much of their time with us. So these were the happy times. Summertime, and the living was easy.

We saw nothing of our maternal relations during our time at The Green, although my mother kept in touch with all her family by post. Presumably even the few shillings which the fare to Oxfordshire would cost became too much for us to visit. But we did have one unexpected visitor.

One summer morning Mary and I were playing on the stile along the lane, when down the hill came a tall and very handsome soldier, swinging a cane. He greeted us a bit stiffly but in the manner of a relation. As well he might, for he was our half-brother Harry.

I remember being a bit awed. Such a handsome young man — and a soldier! He lifted me onto his shoulder, and we showed him the way home. I remember nothing else of his visit, yet surely it must have been a momentous occasion. I think this must have been when he was in the Grenadier Guards. He had joined, as I have said, "to get three square meals a day" — and this was no idle phrase. Such work as he had been able to find had been hard, boring and poorly paid, and (I only learned years afterwards) had brought him to the verge of serious illness when he was with his foster parents. Earlier his headmaster had wanted him to enter for the Grammar School, but of course, there was no question of that; he had to contribute to the family purse at the earliest possible moment. The Army had seemed to him the answer to all his problems. The Recruiting Officer had persuaded him that the Guards was the only place for a tall, upright young fellow like himself, and so he had found himself a slightly surprised Guardsman (not knowing at that time he was following in his own father's footsteps). The reality was harsh, even brutal, and disillusion quickly set in. On this occasion, in the summer of 1930, he was about to embark for India, and we were not to see him for several years.

For us, he was a ship passing. He hardly ever wrote to my mother, apart from a Christmas card or two; I think she rarely knew his address. I am saddened to realise that she probably was less than welcoming when he turned up that day at the Green. A young fellow in his smart uniform, soon to be off to foreign parts, would naturally have expected some expression of affection from his mother. That he had been a great trial to her during the brief periods when he had lived with us may explain some of her coolness, and once when I was grown up she said he "had a vicious tongue" (a trait perhaps inherited from our grandfather, who, I should add, didn't acknowledge his existence). Perhaps at some time he had said something unkind to Mum about the circumstances of his birth. He resented his situation until he died, for it overshadowed his whole life and scarred him permanently. But the trauma of her fall from grace and its attendant horrors had left Mum too with a scar that never healed, and Harry suffered from being a living reminder of it. She hedged when we asked if he really was our brother. Mary said, "I expect he's our foster brother" — it must have been a phrase she'd heard somewhere, and with her innate tact she was throwing our mother a line to grasp, and grasp it she did, gratefully, I felt, and we never mentioned the subject again. Ever.

Of what went on in the outside world during those first Green years I knew very little. Two events stand out, however. When the R 101 airship came to grief, it was the first time I realised that things took place outside our immediate circle and that sometimes the things that happened were awful. Children were much less exposed to the tragedies of life in those pre-television days, when even a wireless set was a fairly rare luxury. We led very sheltered lives (though at the same time we were probably more closely involved with the personal tragedies around us). But somehow we knew about the R 101. Mary, even in those days, was more interested in current affairs than most children of her age, and it was she who decided that we should have a memorial service for the victims of the crash. It was October, and at church we had just had Harvest Festival, so it seemed appropriate to us that the service should have something to do with large marrows and bowls of windfall apples. These we set up on an "altar" of chairs in the back garden. Sammy, Gracie and little Dolly came from next door, and we set our dolls up in a row (including someone's Sunny Jim which had been obtained with Force coupons). Mary conducted the service. We sang "All Things Bright and Beautiful" and said the Lord's Prayer, and Mary recited the poem which begins, "Great big, beautiful, wonderful world . . ."

The relevance of this may have escaped the onlooker, but we were very reverent and solemn, and poor failing Mr White watched us from the window, and confessed to my mother later that he had to wipe away a tear.

The other thing that began to seep into my consciousness was the state of the economy.

Our disagreeable old landlord came for the rent every week, and one day I heard him say (and it was the only mildly thoughtful thing I ever heard him utter): "I'm sorry to hear your husband has been put on short time."

I had realised that my father had been coming home from work earlier of late, and thought it strange and unkind of Mr Smith to be sorry he was no longer having to work so hard. But we had no awareness, yet, of times becoming harder for us. I don't think that it is just with the rosy spectacles of memory that I recall those days with pleasure.

"We had to make our own amusements." The old always say that. It was certainly true, but amusements we had a-plenty. My family were great readers, and we had a good supply of books, and a pile of old Arthur Mee's children's magazines bequeathed to Mary and me by a spinster lady who lived up the lane. These were a source of interest and information throughout our growing years; I have one or two to this day, tattered with much use. From them, I learned at six years old the dying words of Goethe, the story of Benjamin Franklin and his kite, Caxton being visited by Edward IV and his family, as well as better-known events like the death of the Princes in the Tower (complete with pretty Victorian illustrations). And when I had read everything I could lay my hands on, I made up stories for myself, and wrote one or two in an exercise book, to much praise from my parents and dissatisfaction to myself, because I knew they were awful and marvelled that their standards in such matters were so low. Summer days, those cloudless days of childhood, stretched endlessly, full of daisies and buttercups and long, lush grass. We used to walk miles picking wild flowers, sometimes taking a bit of lunch with us. Our mother never seemed to worry that we might be "picked up" and harmed. Once we made a fire and boiled a kettle of water from a rather dubious brook, but we never got around to having our picnic because I fell down a steep bank into a brook and got wet knickers (though

86

whether from the brook or one of my frequent mishaps I can't remember). A car came along and the driver offered us a lift home. We didn't know him, but he had a lady with him, and he explained that this made it all right, but we were never to accept lifts otherwise. (Our mothers had never told us this; cars were so few and far between in our backwater it must have seemed unnecessary.) We accepted, for the sky had darkened and we had gone off the picnic idea. He dropped us off at our gate, and we never saw him and the lady again. Only afterwards we realised they had gone off with my wet knickers.

A social occasion which sticks in my memory is tea with Miss Simms. One day Mary and I, with the Edwards children, were unexpectedly invited to take tea with this lady, a newcomer to The Green (and one of its birds of passage). She was a very respectable lady who had been a nanny of a superior sort — or perhaps a governess, my mother surmised; anyway, there was nothing of the aged retainer about her. We had been strictly instructed on how to behave and, all things considered, conducted ourselves very well, I think, but little Dolly let the side down wanting to wee-wee in the middle of tea (crab apple jelly and seed cake, very refined if unexciting). We looked anxiously at Miss Simms to see if she was shocked. She wasn't. "Like a little tap turned on!" she commented, beaming benignly, as Dolly's performance on the rose-covered chamberpot tinkled all too audibly. I was painfully embarrassed, and would have gone through agonies myself rather than announce my need on such an occasion (unfortunately this happened more than once, with even more embarrassing results).

I suppose Miss Simms must have started her career somewhere around 1880, so looking back now, more than a century later, she appears as a piece of history. She chatted about her former charges. The anecdote which sticks in my mind is one about a girl who desperately wanted a bustle (then the height of fashion). She was considered too young, so she made herself one out of a round biscuit tin.

Poor, lonely Miss Simms, living on her memories. I suppose that little tea party was a rare social occasion for her. I don't ever remember seeing her outside her neat villa, not even at church. But for a long time I treasured the little umbrella-shaped scent bottle I pulled out of her bran tub that afternoon, and I remember her blend of graciousness and sound common sense. I suppose these days she might have made the best kind of social worker. But they don't make her sort any more.

There was a spate of songs at that time which strove to jolly us up in the face of the economic decline which was beginning to darken our lives. (One wonders if there was a Government department in which someone sat up far into the night churning them out.) There were songs about smiling, and sunshine, and rainbows, and counting one's blessings, and good times being around the corner. At home we had a record of a manly baritone singing a song called (would you believe?) "Prosperity Will Soon Be Here Again":

. . . We don't want another war
But this is one worth fighting for,
Prosperity will soon be here again!

None of this un-British whining about "Buddies Sparing a Dime", you will note.

Thus armed, we went into the Depression.

CHAPTER
FOUR

Tumbledown Dick's

The Green was respectable, as hamlets go, and by the yardstick by which such things may be measured, the Tye was not. If, as I think the Bible insists, "Happy is the man who hath his quiver full", the Tye had more than its share of happy men. They didn't look very happy, as I recall them, but then, about half the population was out of work, and the combination of poverty and full quivers, in the days before Child Allowances, must have made life difficult — though it was the women who had the grey hairs. The Bible doesn't say a lot about the happiness of women.

We moved to the Tye in October 1931. My father transported me on the crossbar of his bike, the cat hanging out of a box at the back, meowing pitifully.

Old Mr Smith had put his own house on the market, and wanted to live in ours. I don't think that even he would have cast us into the road — though I don't know if a tenant had much in the way of legal protection in those days. But the question didn't arise, because our milkman, who was a small local farmer called Randall, offered us an old cottage which had previously accommodated one of his labourers. My parents accepted — they had no choice — but my mother hated it from the first moment, and never felt comfortable in it. It had been, long ago and probably far into the Victorian era, an alehouse. The building was said to be fifteenth century (I later learned), and nowadays is the kind of place photographed by tourists and pictured on calendars. In those days, it was considered shaming among the working classes to live in a thatched cottage. "That owd thatched place," the locals would say contemptuously. And certainly we never told anyone what it was called — Tumbledown Dick's, presumably called after Oliver Cromwell's poor inadequate son or the old country game (which came first, I wonder?). Nowadays, a name like that is emblazoned with pride on the gatepost, and probably adds a couple of thousand to the asking price. We didn't need a detailed address; we alone of all the hamlet had a surname which, though common enough, wasn't shared with at least one other family.

Our cottage had formed one side of an L-shaped courtyard, with a row of crumbling cottages on the other, but at the time we moved in, the latter were in the process of being knocked down as uninhabitable. The former residents, families like the Shiptons and Wickses and Fowlers, had been moved to the new Council houses in Lucketts Lane, up the road and across the green. My mother would have liked a Council house, with what passed for mod. cons. in those days, but I don't think she — or we — would ever really have fitted in. There were no "outsiders" in

Lucketts Lane, and wherever we lived, we were outsiders.

We, of course, had no mod. cons. at all, unless you counted the cold water tap at the gate (or where the gate would have been if we had one; we seemed doomed to go through our lives gateless). Every drop we used had to be carried up the garden path in buckets, and in winter it froze. It goes without saying there was no bathroom; we had a hip bath, which was quite snug in front of the fire on a Saturday night, and Mary and I (and, after we were in bed, our Mother) used the same water. Mary was fastidious, and hated me to use it first, as I invariably did; she didn't trust my notoriously unreliable bladder ("Good for the complexion," said Mother). There was no sink, no drain, so emptying the bath was as backbreaking as filling it. Visiting the lavatory after dark was an adventure not to be undertaken lightly. We had two lavatories (for the house had previously been divided into two dwellings); one was older and more smelly (I can well believe it was the original) and the other, which we normally used in the early days, was picturesquely situated on a sort of little peninsular jutting out into the pond, so you had to watch your step in the dark.

To begin with, our rent was five shillings a week. For this we had a small living room from which opened a scullery exposed to the naked thatch, so that the birds in their nests tended to deposit feathers and droppings from a height onto the floor beneath, and sometimes onto cooking utensils and food that had been left for a moment uncovered. For cooking there was an ancient iron grate in the living room, which was a haven for crickets, and their chirrupings were the accompaniment to our winter evenings, causing my mother some distress, because she classed them with bugs. Along the little dark passage there was a cold, T-shaped cave-room which presumably had served the pub as a cellar, and beyond was the former taproom. The brick floor was worn with the feet of centuries, with little hollows where the drinkers of yore had regularly stood. The fireplace filled most of one wall, and there was no hearth as such. The chimney was enormous and went straight up, with iron staples in the sides for the poor little chimney sweeps (or Father Christmas). Around the inner walls of the hearth were little apertures at elbow height where the drinkers could leave their ale to warm. In the corner of this room there was a staircase in a cupboard, leading to one bedroom, but the bedrooms we occupied were over the living room and cellar, approached by another dark little stair leading off the passage. My parents' room was, like the scullery, open to the thatch, with the same disadvantages, and with additional ones — the comings and goings of nocturnal wildlife. The little room I shared with Mary was next to it, with a tiny dormer casement, and adjoining this, though boarded up, windowless and impossible to enter, was another room. We speculated uncomfortably as to what horrors the room might contain, but we never did solve the mystery. But I think it bothered our mother; she confessed later that when we had gone to school she used to dash upstairs and make the beds and tidy round, and then go back down and try not to think of it again all day.

I think during this time she must have been very low and depressed, probably not helped by a poor diet and constant money worries, plus the worries of my father's increasing difficulties, which were both self-inflicted and pressed on him by the world outside. It is to their eternal credit that we children suspected very little of this. To us, ours was a happy home, full of warmth and love and security. If we ever suspected that something was wrong, I for one had a great talent for self-deception. Mary was older, and more sensitive, and I think she must have sometimes worried.

At least at the Tye there would never be a problem about "Keeping up with the Joneses" (not that our family had ever had that problem). Most of us were in the same boat. One or two families were just above the breadline, with the man of the house having a job, and perhaps a teenage offspring or two contributing. My mother became friendly with a Mrs Johnson, who certainly considered herself a bit superior to the average Tye resident, coming from Edmonton and not having rent to pay, because her husband had built them a nice wooden bungalow and made a comfortable living as a freelance carpenter. Her sister and brother-in-law kept the pub, and another brother-in-law kept the little shop on the green. We already knew the pub people, because we had sometimes come on a Sunday evening in the course of our ritual stroll. On the first occasion, Dad had put out his usual feelers towards the landlord to see if there was any point of contact, and somehow the

phrase "Grandma and Lucky Jim" had cropped up —
one wonders how, but strange and devious were my
father's tactics. Comradeship was immediately established,
for those had been the names of two of the big guns
operating during the late war in which both men had
served.

After that, there was no stopping them. I can see
now, with hindsight and pity, that most of the men who
suffered indescribably in those dreadful years must
have moved through the early years of "peace" with a
sense of unreality and confusion, like men released
from a madhouse, and only in the company of those
who had shared their experiences could they feel
relaxed and "at home". Relax they did, the landlord
and my father; both got very drunk, and we had to steer
Dad home with care afterwards, because in his state of
euphoria he insisted on walking in the middle of the
road and got hit by a lightless bicycle.

Mrs Johnson and her sisters were very dark; so was
Peggy, the sole offspring of the Johnson marriage. She
was a year younger than Mary, a doted-on child whose
aunts knitted her pretty angora woollies and bought her
doll's prams and miniature house furniture. She was
spoilt, but not unpleasant. Her "only child" state was
much envied. Her mother was a "strong" woman,
confident of her own charm and ability. The Johnson
household was a ménage à trois, for they had a lodger.
Mr Johnson was a sober, haggard man who seemed to
have never quite recovered from the war, but in a
quieter, less obvious way than my father. He didn't
really seem to count for much in the eyes of his

womenfolk, poor man, and he knew it. He liked to talk to my mother in a sad, worried sort of way. What a contrast was their paying guest! Uncle Oz was not, of course, an uncle at all. He was big and charming and jolly, good with children and bubbling with self-confidence. Young though I was, I had figured out something of the situation, and I couldn't help thinking how superfluous Mr Johnson was. Peggy and her mother hardly seemed to notice him at all.

Next door to us on the west side lived an old couple called Blackstone. They were little, white-haired, and like many of their age group, never wore anything but black. The old lady never appeared outside the house, except to stand occasionally at the front step, and Mr B. never went outside the garden. Mum was always telling us not to make too much noise, but I think he liked to see us running around, and his whole life seemed to revolve around our doings, for he stood ("lurked", we said) behind the hedge, particularly interested in me, it seemed; "the lesser 'un" was how he referred to me. No-one, then, seemed to find this slightly suspicious behaviour, and perhaps it wasn't. They had no surviving children, and their lives must have been bleak. How they managed financially I can't imagine. I think the pension was only ten shillings each a week, and they couldn't have saved much, though he wasn't a drinking man; all he asked of life was his "bit o' baccy".

Beyond their cottage was a little Victorian house occupied by Miss Sarah Barker and her unmarried brother. Perhaps she was no more than fifty-ish; to us she seemed very old, and prim, and neat, with an aspidistra and lace curtains, always twitching, for she liked to observe all comings and goings. The only person she ever spoke to, except of necessity, was my mother, who fielded her prying enquiries with some dexterity and amusement. Poor Sarah, she was a figure of fun to us children. But she did have a wireless a bit later, on which (she said) she only listened to the news and the church services. (It may even have been true.) Though there was little enough on the B.B.C. to offend even the most delicately nurtured maiden lady.

Beyond the Barkers was the little Mission Hall — of which more later. There were one or two detached villas farther down the lane, occupied by a retired shopkeeper and an ex-accountant, and then opposite us was a biggish (by hamlet standards) enclosed house where the Frank Northwoods lived; they owned the market garden which employed several of the local males — indeed, were the only source of employment at the Tye. They had no children, which was considered locally either very selfish or very sad — and downright odd in that community of full quivers. Mrs Frank was a nice, quiet woman, for whom Mum later did a bit of occasional cleaning. Sadly, she was killed in a motor accident a few years later.

Thus we could be said to live at the more respectable end of the green, being some distance from the Council houses. But the family that let the side down was the Tadgells. They lived in a battered thatched cottage on the other side of the pub, surrounded by a scraggy vegetable patch (no space was wasted on namby-pamby nonsense like flowers, not with all those mouths to feed). A few scraggy hens scratched around in the dust, and three or four half-starved cats, usually off-white and one-eared, lay listlessly on windowsills. I only once saw inside the Tadgell kitchen and was shocked to find that there was no floor — not just no carpet or lino, but quite literally no floor. Either the beaten earth was all there had ever been, or the floorboards had been taken up at some time, for firewood, perhaps. Always there were little male Tadgells sitting around on the floor or in the yard, usually wearing a non-descript greyish garment which may have been a vest. The lower half was usually unclothed, and I was shocked to see that all the little boys suffered from a curious growth in a very private place. I never mentioned this fact to anyone, not even Mary, so perhaps even at that tender age I may have suspected that I could be getting it wrong.

Mr Tadgell was out of work. I can't believe that he had ever been in work, for his movements were so slow that I can't think of any job for which he might have been suited. He was said to beat his children mercilessly. They certainly kept out of his way as much as possible; there was no difficulty about that during opening hours (no wonder there was no money to buy his small sons trousers).

Mrs Tadgell wasn't quite the poor browbeaten creature she might have been, nor, despite her large family, was there anything of the earth mother about her. She was quite spirited really, and always on the move, in contrast to almost every other member of the family — including the livestock. She was in her thirties, I suppose, but the years had taken more than their toll. She was like a scarecrow, spare, with a wildly flapping look about her. Her hair was always escaping from its pins and her dentures gave her a lot of trouble, as though they had been made for someone else — as perhaps they had. Her voice was strident, and when raised, as it often was, had a touch of the eldritch in it. Most of her yelling was at the unfortunate Elvira: "You El-vee-ra! Come 'ere!" Elvira, at ten years old or so, was the oldest of the family, and physically like her mother, but with a more anxious look. Poor girl, she was never allowed to be a child, for she was the household drudge, and had to run all the way home from school every day to spend as much time as possible at her mother's side, fetching and carrying, minding the little ones, preparing the evening meal. I never did see her play, not once. I say she was the oldest; there had been at least one child before her, who had died at about six months (so Doris told me with gloomy relish). I should think it was from gastro-enteritis, judging by the feeding bottles I saw in the hands of the littlest Tadgells. But it is not to be thought of that in large, inadequate families the death of a baby was something that didn't matter. The baby was remembered and spoken of by name (which was Nola) by the brothers and sisters who hadn't known her. (Lucky Nola, one is tempted to think, seeing what was happening to Elvira).

Like everyone else, Mrs Tadgell wanted to be my mother's friend, to Mum's great embarrassment.

My mother, as I have indicated, was just a little bit of a snob in some ways — not a money snob, certainly, nor a social position snob. She respected intelligence — not necessarily "cleverness" or education, for she herself had neither, but simple sense and sensitivity. She liked instinctive good manners, and she liked people who could talk about things other than the doings of their neighbours. She despised self-pity, and gossip, and ignorant narrowness (though in the years of my childhood she was surprisingly rigid in some of her views). She never felt really comfortable with extroverts. I don't know whether Mrs Tadgell could be called an extrovert; apart from her unwelcome calls on my mother I never saw her outside her own domain. I never really listened to her conversation; I only remember that it was conducted very loudly and forcefully to the accompaniment of clashing dentures. She once brought Mum a large jar of cod liver oil and malt which the District Nurse had given her for the children, but they "turned up their noses at it", and she thought it would be good for me and Mary. Mum bridled, though she accepted with stiff courtesy so as not to offend. I can imagine her feelings about the suggestion that her children needed handouts more than the little Tadgells; and she never gave it to us. To accept something from Mrs Tadgell, something at which the Tadgell children had turned up their noses, was beneath her dignity. Anything from that household bore a stigma. It must be covered in germs.

When I became friendly with Doris, my mother disapproved (as she had disapproved of the Bardoes).

100

But she said very little. She was uneasy if Doris came into the house to wait for me, and watched suspiciously, for things tended to disappear when Doris was around. Sweets, few enough in our house at the best of times, became even fewer after a visit from Doris; she would have made a marvellous conjuror. But it was the fear of nits that made my mother jumpy. Perhaps, long ago, the Tadgell children had had their hair washed. Perhaps beneath their muddy-beige colouring (hair, skin, teeth, were all the same) there lay glowing Saxon gold. I have felt, since, that Doris may have grown up a real stunner, and one way or another got her money's worth out of life. I hope so.

Throughout the time we lived at the Tye, her brother Stanley was in love with me. I didn't need telling that this was so. The other children on the coal lorry teased him mercilessly, and he blushed to the grimy roots of his hair. When they discovered that I too was embarrassed, nay, mortified, they had a field day — many field days; the torment lasted two or three years. (Reading *Sunnybrook Farm*, which Mary and I loved, we recognised immediately the improvident neighbouring family with the gangling son who had a crush on Rebecca — it was the Tadgells to a T.)

If Mr Tadgell had a profession, he was a poacher. I suppose he must have been quite good at it, for the children often had a rabbit dinner, or a pheasant if the local gamekeeper was looking the other way, so perhaps they were better nourished than they looked — better, indeed, than we were. He overstepped the mark at least once, however, when he acquired a chicken from someone's farmyard. I suppose there had been other offences on record, for local opinion was that "it would be prison this time", but in view of his circumstances, he was allowed off with a fine — though how he was to pay a fine when he was too poor to support his family without stealing wasn't explained.

Strangely, in so crowded a household, the Tadgells had a lodger, Mr Gaylor, who was — or had been — a roadman. His own standards can't have been too high, but I think the existence of a paying guest gave the Tadgells a little status symbol, as well as an additional income. He wasn't often visible, and I have no idea how he spent his days if he was no longer employed. He had a daughter, Dolly, who lived and worked in London — probably in one of the north-eastern garment factories. I see her in retrospect rather like Hardy's Ruined Maid, for she was delightfully and unashamedly common. She was the first woman about whom I heard the word applied, and I knew immediately what it meant. I thought her very pretty and smart, with her red lips and crimped yellow hair with a beret almost vertical upon it, running jerkily in her high heels, dropping daffodils as she ran after a Sunday visit to her father. She shouted to my father as she passed, "I've bin on the cadge!" referring presumably to the daffodils; she would have been hard put to cadge anything else from the Tye at that time.

Apart from Dolly, and the London relations of the pub people, and our own in their season, visitors to the hamlet were rare. Unwelcome ones who came in the spring and autumn were a band of gypsies who made camp at the end of the lane beyond the Johnsons' bungalow. I don't know if they were real gypsies. There would be a couple of caravans and some piebald ponies and a horde of disagreeable-looking children who either shied away from us or threw stones. No wonder they were hostile; nobody wanted them, and there was no encouragement for them to be other than dirty and defensive. The hamlet parents regarded them with fear and loathing, which must have been their lot for centuries.

My mother's and Mrs Johnson's objection was based on firmer ground than mere mindless prejudice: dirt meant disease. There was some basis for their unease, for one year there was said to be scarlet fever at the camp, and the Health people moved in and carried off the victims. And once their "chief" lay dying — I don't know of what — and we passed the shelter which had been erected where he lay (a tent which was just a tarpaulin thrown over a rough frame) and saw him propped up, covered by old coats, staring listlessly out at us, while his "clan" gathered outside in eerie silence, glaring at us as we passed. We spent the rest of the day in sombre mood on Peggy's doorstep, talking of death and bereavement.

Interestingly, in view of our mothers' preoccupation with the infectiousness of the Tadgells, I never remember any of them losing a day's schooling through ill health — well, only once, on a Monday, and when my mother asked Doris the reason, she answered: "We all had rhubarb Sunday and we had to have flour." And when I did catch nits, it was from a very respectable cousin.

With money becoming ever scarcer, our parents still managed to give us little treats. Christmas was, as always, magical — perhaps even more so in that atmospheric old house with the enormous chimney open to the stars, and the hearth across which my father dragged a real Yule log. This burned throughout the two or three days of the festival, glowing aromatically, which, along with the smell of candlewax and orange peel, still sets my memory buds tingling.

We loved the build-up to the great celebration almost more than the event itself. I remember that we children started getting the Christmas feeling somewhere around Harvest Thanksgiving — that is, about the time our mothers put us in our winter combinations and wool stockings. I recall with warm delight the smell of apples and chrysanthemums and paraffin lamps, and the feeling that ". . . all was safely gathered in . . ." We welcomed the nip in the air that came soon after. Then Hallowe'en — not the Americanised version with its unpleasant undertones which has crept in recently, but a simple giggly affair at which we bobbed for apples by candlelight. Then All Saints and my birthday, and Bonfire Night, and Advent ("O come, O come, Emmanuel" in the choir, and mothers making the Christmas puddings and letting us have a stir to wish on). Then Christmas cards of course — not the big, meaningless ritual they have since become; each one sent and received was savoured, each a delight (and delivered right up to Christmas morning). I suppose our family's total was about a dozen each way — and many of our acquaintances received and sent fewer, and never to people they saw often. As a child I sent one card each year, to a little friend in Oxfordshire; she never sent back because her mother said cards were a waste of money (mine usually cost a ha'penny, with a ha'penny for a stamp if sent unsealed). My mother sent to her brother and sisters, one or two old friends and to such aunts as remained. She always sent a shilling to her old Aunt Annie, wrapped in cotton wool, and to her mother she sent an apron (bought from the tallyman and paid for by the week). That, with a bit of tobacco for my grandfather, was the extent of her Christmas giving, and even that was a generosity she could ill afford at times.

School broke up quite close to Christmas Eve, and how good it was, that last afternoon, with no work insisted on, the classroom decked with homemade paperchains, and the teachers in unnaturally jocular mood (which made us slightly uneasy). We each got an orange and a few little booklets and puzzles issued from firms like Shredded Wheat: ("the Factory in a Garden" — i.e., Welwyn Garden City) and we giggled a lot, and the boys threw paper pellets without getting told off, while the short December day faded outside and the teachers pulled on the hissing gaslamps, reminding us uncomfortably (yet thrillingly) that it would be dark before we got home.

From the age of eight, I was allowed to go carol singing with Mary and our friend Peggy. We wriggled with excitement as my mother lighted the candle in the triangular lantern and, bundled up in scarves and mittens, we set out into the darkness. Peggy was a giggler; Mary took it very seriously, as I did. We gave real value for money, and became quite well-known for it. Not for us the old hackneyed ones, "Good King Wenceslas" and "While Shepherds Watched"; these were the basic repertoire of the Lucketts Lane lot, who didn't take the business seriously at all, but belted out one verse and thumped on the door. They jeered at us for actually enjoying singing, and we gave them a wide berth when we could. We felt quite insulted if a door opened before we had given them the full treatment. My own favourite, because it was jolly, was "God Rest Ye, Merry Gentlemen". I remember we sang that at the door of a notoriously disagreeable farmer called Dunhill. We felt very nervous making our way through the darkly-hedged pathway to the door, trying not to let him suspect our approach until we could start mellowing him with our singing. Off we went, but when we got to the bit about ". . . embracing in love and brotherhood . . ." the vision of Mr Dunhill embracing anybody, even Mrs Dunhill, was too much. Peggy dissolved into giggles and infected me — so much that I became quite hysterical and collapsed into the bushes just as the formidable Dunhill opened the door. Mary, who had finished the performance as a solo, was equal to the situation, accepted his shilling (a shilling!) graciously, bade him the compliments of the season, and covered our disorderly retreat with dignity. Split three ways, our takings usually amounted to about half a crown or three shillings each; not bad, considering the economic climate of the time — for we never approached the poorer households, and sometimes covered three miles to collect this. Added to our "savings" (largesse from summer visitors) it made a nice little sum for Christmas presents, decorations, and other seasonable goodies.

Going into town to do our Christmas shopping was a great thrill. The occasion I most clearly remember was a market day, after school, and dark. It must have been before my father became unemployed, because we met him from his place of work. He took charge of me while my mother and Mary went off to do their shopping. He took me to buy fruit at the stalls, which at that time must have carried out their business far into the evening, as did the shops. I found the scene quite magical, all the piles of waxy, gleaming fruit, especially the tangerines, pyramids of orange and silver. (Fruit, I may say, was something of a luxury in our house.) All touched with enchantment in the light from the gas flares, which hissed and flared fitfully in the chilling wind. Then we moved on to Woolworth's.

Woolworth's at Christmas must loom large in any pre-war child's memory — Woolworth's at any time, for that matter, for it was always magic, and no town was considered a town without that red and gold shopfront with the legend "Nothing Over Sixpence" comfortingly emblazoned. We never thought the day would come when dear old Woollies would put up the shutters in High Street after High Street. In the 1930s it seemed that it would go on forever, a part of the urban scenery like fish and chips and Co-ops and Home and

Colonials. To say that to a child entering Woolworth's at Christmas was like entering Aladdin's cave may be trite but was the very truth. Who can forget the smell, and the brown floorboards which, though bare, had a curious softness? My earliest impression was of a forest of legs, through which one fought like the prince in Sleeping Beauty crashing through the undergrowth. Then at eye level were the counters, and what a feast they were! Particularly at Christmas I loved the counter selling paper chains and Christmas tree baubles, a riot of colour. And it was probably here that I first saw Christmas wrapping paper; until then, presents had come modestly wrapped in brown paper and string. This new paper had a design of holly on it (there was only one) and the notice said: "Make Your Gifts Look Christmassy!" (I heard someone say, "What will they think of next to part you from your money!") It was many years before the idea took off in our family, being considered a wild extravagance.

Coming out into the cold and crowded street, I had the only uneasy moment of that memorable evening. This was at the sight of a poor old man pathetically dragging himself along in a travesty of Father Christmas robes, all hunched up against the cold, a picture of wretchedness, trying unsuccessfully to sell tawdry little toys from a tray. It occurs to me that he may have been an old soldier. At the time, I didn't question my father, but wrestled in private with my confusion and sadness. But the image haunted me, and haunts me still.

108

After shopping we walked home — that is, my parents and sister walked; I sat on my father's bike and he pushed me. The distance was, I think, about five miles, and the road almost without houses once the lights of the town were behind us. The darkness seemed absolute; there was no moon, nor stars, and only the flickering little oil lamp on the bike to show us where the road was. I was comfortable enough, snug and protected with my father's arm supporting me, and the dark held no terrors with him and Mum beside me. I think we only met one vehicle on the journey, and the only lights were the rare glimmer from a cottage or two, well back from the road, and a farmyard where a dog barked as we passed. We could, of course, have caught a bus to the village and walked the mere two-and-a-half miles from there; I suppose the cost would have been no more than one-and-sixpence for the three of us — Dad biking home as he normally did — but one-and-six saved was one-and-six more to spend on Christmas goodies, and that was fine with Mary and me.

For the two days of Christmas, life was unreal. The magic didn't end with the revelations of Christmas morning and the exciting rustle on the bed as we moved our waking feet ("He's been!") At that moment we conveniently forgot that we hadn't got the fairy cycle we'd asked for, nor the talking doll. Everything was "just what we wanted", down to the apple, orange and nuts at the foot of our sagging stockings, still with their magical aura from their ride through the frosty air. At mealtimes, and even in between, overeating was not only allowed but actually encouraged, to make up for the rest of the year when belt-tightening was a necessary virtue. Neighbours popped in, the Johnsons and Randall the landlord with his young son, a pair of Johnson cousins and the jovial Uncle Oz, and every Christmas for many years a young man from the old cracker factory who brought us the most luxurious crackers with lovely things inside — which I didn't appreciate because I was always afraid of things that went Bang. The evening entertainment included games of Banker, played for matches (unless Christmas fell on a Sunday), and more boisterous amusements like Blind Man's Buff, and Squeak Piggy Squeak, in all of which grown-ups and children joined. My father operated the wind-up gramophone and played records like "When You Walk Up High Street, Africa" and "Ali Barber's Camel", singing along with enthusiasm. There was, as far as I remember, very little in the way of food and drink dispensed at these gatherings; a glass of beer for the men, perhaps, and ginger wine and a mince pie for the ladies — though it must be said that Dad usually managed to get fairly well lubricated offstage. He didn't get maudlin until the end of Boxing Day, when harsh reality was staring us in the face and all the nuts and oranges were eaten, and we sat close to the fire as the old Yule log crumbled and the room grew dark and cold. Then he would sing "Oh, but I'm longing for my Ain Folk" and other songs from his Scottish repertoire, and deep melancholy would settle on us, and I would think of going back to school and of the bleak grey days

110

and the long, long weeks until Easter, and the prospect seemed too awful to be borne.

I remember being told at school, in the Infants, that we should practice our reading at home, and read the papers. So, at seven years old, I picked out a piece at random; it was about the miners.

"Fancy filling a child's head with that sort of stuff!" said my mother when I pestered her for enlightenment. For I didn't understand a word, yet what came through to me was that the miners were not very happy.

Just after that my father lost his job. During the rest of his working life I learned to recognise the signs when he had got the sack. He would come into the house in a dragging sort of way, and with a grey look about him. He'd sit down and put off as long as possible the awful news, while my mother, sensing and dreading what was to come, clattered the teacups and pretended she didn't know. Then she'd sit down and they'd face each other. He'd say, "I've got put off," and I'd see her stricken look that melted into pity for him; she knew how his self-esteem was suffering. She'd pull herself together then, bustle a bit and give him a cup of tea, and put his meal in front of him. He'd push it aside and she'd talk him into eating "just a bit" and, "We'll manage," she'd say. She was so good, so supportive, putting on a brave face when weeks, months — years, for all she knew — of grinding poverty lay before her, when even in the "good" times it had been hard enough to make ends meet.

There were times in those lean years when even my mother almost reached the end of her tether. There was one week when, no matter how she schemed and juggled, there was no way of making our twenty-eight shillings cover our outgoings. She said, later, it was the only time in her married life when she came very close to despair. She threw down her pencil and said to my father, "It's no good. I can't manage." He loved to tell how he had picked up the pencil and went through every item on her list. At the end, he balanced the books with a penny over. They had a ha'penny each (but I think that must have been a bitter joke).

Yet in all that time she would never touch my father's pension, which he got for his near-useless hand. He got four shillings a week for that from our grateful government; that was his beer and tobacco money.

He had never earned much, but our lifestyle was simple, and with Mum being the good manager that she was, we never felt deprived. Of course, I realise now that our parents often went without in order that our growing bodies might have most of what they needed, and a little bit extra when it could be managed. I remember my father reading aloud from the "Letters" page of *John Bull* (that, and the *Daily Herald*, were an accepted luxury — my parents would rather have gone without a meal than a paper). An out-of-work father was describing how they saved the jam for their children while he and his wife "looked at the pretty picture on the jar". I'm sure my mother despised that as self-pity, but no doubt she and my father could have said the same sort of thing.

Certain sacrifices she wouldn't make: she wouldn't use margarine except for cooking; it was linked in her mind with the deprivations of the past war, and of course, it wasn't the pleasant-tasting product we have now. Strange, then, that she never used eggs for cake making. Living in the country one would think that eggs would have been part of out basic diet. Not so; they were an occasional Sunday morning treat or a substitute main meal, and for cooking she used some stuff called "Golden Rising Powder", for the indigestible rock cakes she made on Sundays, and for puddings, and to bolster the infrequent scrambled eggs. We rarely had milk, except in our tea and cocoa and on our porridge, and then it was used sparingly. Somewhere around this time, school milk was introduced (perhaps the idea came from the same think-tank that had inspired the post-Great War baby clinics). We considered this a great treat. For a ha'penny — half the usual retail price — we got a third of a pint at morning break, and I think there may have been help for large impoverished families, along with a double helping for at least one girl who was very pale and may have been the offspring of a consumptive parent. (However large our family or frail our physiques, I can't imagine our Mum accepting this sort of "charity"; she'd have found the money somehow. As it was, she considered the fivepence a week well spent, and we preened ourselves as she promised that we would now grow up healthy and beautiful. Sadly, it didn't work in either case.)

Mary and I had no consciousness of being very poor. That we never had new clothes was no surprise; few of our peers did, except Peggy. But there was always food of some sort on our table, mostly stew of the less digestible kind, admittedly, and the meat uneatable, and when my mother thought we should have a change she would make what she called "a good old bacon pudding"; the phrase was to jolly us up, for it wasn't good at all, it was awful, a big roll of suet pastry with tiny scraps of streaky bacon, which I was pressed to eat because it would "grease my chest" (my mother was very keen on lubricating my chest, inside and out). But somehow we usually managed to have a roast dinner on Sundays. I don't know how this ritual was maintained, but I do know it was important to Mum.

And it wasn't as extravagant as it might appear. My father biked into town and bought it at Dewhursts, the village shop being too expensive for the likes of us. I think it usually cost about three and sixpence, and for that we ate well, the four of us, for two days, with something left over for sandwiches to take to school. For the rest of the week, there was always cheese for me and fishpaste, dripping, potato or mustard (!) for Mary. Some of the hamlet children took bread and sugar to school, but that never appealed to us. And we always had butter. If the Lucketts Lane lot had butter ("best butter" they called it) instead of the usual marge, they didn't expect to get anything else with it, and thought Mary and me very pampered and toffee-nosed because we got "best butter" every day, as well as something on it. "And your Dad on the dole like everyone else's," they said, wonderingly.

Our great salvation was a constant supply of fresh vegetables, home grown, of course. The soil in our

114

garden was rich and dark, like wedding cake, having been well-nourished over the centuries like our grandfather's. All the hamlet men were good gardeners. As countrymen they had to be, and were brought up so from an early age. Even quite young boys had their own vegetable plot. My father was exceptional only in his love of flowers. He never lost his city child's wonder at these, and was proud of his dahlias and rows of bedding plants that filled our front garden in their season, and indeed, he was rather a bore on the subject. Most of the local men either didn't bother with flowers or left it to their wives to "stick a few bits in" by the front door, this concession granted in a slightly jocular way: "Keeps the owd gal happy." Otherwise, their attitude was summed up by the reasoning: "If you can't put it on a plate, why grow it?" My father thought there ought to be more to life than that.

Our daily bread was very good indeed. It was baked and brought to us by Mr Fritz. He was German, which confused me more than somewhat, for my mental picture of "the Hun" was of the nightmarish, strangely-helmeted enemy I saw in my father's war books. Mr Fritz had ginger hair and a little moustache, and he was cheery and talkative and had hardly any accent. He had been taken a prisoner of war and brought to England, and when the war ended had had the good sense to marry a local girl whose father ran a business in the same trade as his own. He now ran the bakery himself, a very satisfactory arrangement, for his bread was said to be the best for miles around. He became something of a friend to my parents, as all our tradesmen did, and he chose some strange times to come and collect his money. If my father was at home, they would sit down and talk about the war, and politics, and life in general, and if Dad was at the pub, then Mr Fritz would sit and talk to Mum quite happily.

I remember one occasion, a Saturday night, when I was plagued with boils and came downstairs to find him sitting by the fire cosily with Mum (quite decorously, I hasten to add — though one might wonder) and he sympathised with my plight and jollied me up while Mum prepared and applied an excruciating hot bread poultice.

Other tradesmen came and lingered and talked. Mr Randall, of course, was as much a friend as a landlord and milkman. He was a "character", ugly, tough, hardworking, and nobody's fool. Not an intellectual, even by Tye standards, and his interests were not my parents', and if he had any political preferences, they would not have been my father's, now he had "crossed the floor". But he liked a chat, and we had an affection, of sorts, for him, and our paths were destined to draw closer for a while.

Then there was Mr Bill Walters. He was a tallyman, that now extinct species, killed off by the growth of the mail order business. In those days, the tallyman performed an essential service, successors in their turn to the old itinerant pedlars who had done so much for scattered communities, more than just supplying goods. Mum bought our shoes from Mr Walters. Shoes were the one item she wouldn't let us inherit, conscious of her own lifelong troubles from that source. And she occasionally bought household articles like bedlinen — and even, once, a bed, to replace the little single one which Mary and I had shared and from which I was always falling out. I assume this must have committed her to more than at the usual shilling or two a week — half a crown, perhaps, which must have taken some finding. Before Mr Walters there had been a Mrs Watts, a voluble, businesslike woman who kept my mother informed of the births, deaths, insolvencies and illicit affairs within a radius of fifteen miles. (My mother didn't want to know, and was always uncomfortable when Mrs Watts was in full spate — but that may have been because her conversation wasn't always suitable for little pricked-up ears.) Mr Walters took over her round, and we enjoyed his visits, which he enjoyed even more, I think, for his home life was far from satisfactory, and he loved to settle down with a cup of tea and pour out his troubles — though this in a lively and even amusing manner. He was a garrulous, breezy man, a gifted raconteur, and he regaled us with tales of his adventures in the wild East End, where he went, once a week, to the warehouse. Our world was so small, it was all fascinating stuff to us. Particularly I recall his account of a brief encounter with C. B. Cochrane's Young Ladies, the ultimate in showbiz glamour in those days. On this occasion they had been in the East End on some publicity stunt. I listened wide-eyed to Mr Walters' description of their clothes and hair and make-up: "Their eyelids were all blue and their faces were this sort of sun-tan — in November!" I lapped it up, thinking, "that's for me when I grow up . . ."

Mr Walters' light-hearted chatter hid a heavy heart. He had lost an adored little daughter, and my parents' sympathy was aroused, perhaps in part because they felt they had almost lost a child themselves. The tragedy had turned Mrs Walters' brain, and she did nothing in the house and refused to eat, saying that all her food turned to glass — though there was evidence that she raided the pantry in the night. I don't suppose there was much in the way of help for bereaved families in those days. Many people had turned their backs on the religion which had consoled their Victorian predecessors, and the fashion for "counselling" was years away. In summer, Dad used to select a bunch of his special white dahlias for the little girl's grave, and this used to bring poor Mr Walters to the verge of tears.

Even his daughter's death and his wife's depression wasn't the whole of the tragedy. Ten years or so later I read in the local paper that he had hanged himself. He was working as a hospital porter then, his itinerant days over. I think he must have died of his long grief, and remembering how full of life he had always seemed, we felt immensely saddened.

I don't know whether my father's conversion to Socialism was gradual or sudden. He had been such a staunch Tory, and intensely loyal to all things British. He had a great affection, too, for the Royal Family, especially Queen Mary, who had inspected the British Legion in Hyde Park when he was present in the front rank at an Armistice Day parade (there was, I think, some sort of lottery among the local branches for this honour), when she, seeing so many ageing and disabled men who had once been patriotic boys, had tears running down her face. She made no attempt to wipe them away, he said.

Armistice Day was an occasion to be dreaded, year after year, ending always with the ritual drowning of memories — which he nevertheless hugged to his heart with a sort of masochism; and we all suffered with him.

I remember those still November days, and the two minutes' silence being religiously observed, with all vehicles stopping and everyone downing tools, men standing, heads bowed, caps in hand. How eerie it was, that grey, dripping silence. I remember trooping out from school and along the wet street, standing with our feet among the wet leaves, dimly and dutifully sad. I remember the blood-red poppies against the grey stone of the memorial where the names were, and the heart-aching, sick-making hymns "Oh valiant hearts, who to your glory came . . ." Beautiful, but the "glory" didn't match up with my father's memories of mud and limbless corpses and poor, frightened boys. I would think of my poor little Uncle Bert, and force my heart into a burst of personal grief.

Dad's pride and pleasure in being British never really left him, but the treatment meted out to the severely disadvantaged during the Depression made him see red — literally.

I remember a rep. from one of the national papers calling on my mother one day, trying to persuade her to order something like the *Daily Mail* or the *Daily Express*, but she said No, her husband had only just changed his allegiance and was unlikely to change again. It was true; he remained faithful to the *Daily Herald* (the Labour paper) from that time until it folded many years later. The significance hardly touched me at the time, but three or four years later it was brought home to me at school, when the Headmaster asked each of us which paper, if any, our fathers read (it was assumed that women weren't interested in newspapers). It strikes me now as a pretty sneaky thing to do, but the object of the exercise is all too clear. When he came to me, I alone admitted to the *Herald*, and thought nothing of it, until I realised that he was fixing me with a stare of quickened interest. I remember him murmuring "Does he, by Jove!"and felt that by my admission I had become suspect, the daughter of a wild revolutionary, conspicuous among that class of politically uninterested children, brought up to subscribe, like their parents, to what was basically a feudal system — the village was feudal, for half the children were the offspring of the gentry's servants or their tenants, and the other half the children of their tradesmen, or were in some other ways influenced by the pervading gentility of the village. From that time, I never felt the Head was entirely comfortable with me. He ignored me as much as possible (I'm not sure if this also applied to Mary; she had left school by the time of the newspaper incident). He never gave me the sort of encouragement that might have led me to try for Grammar School; the only hamlet children thus honoured were Farmer Randall's John and the daughter of the butcher who lived beyond the Green. As it happened, that suited me very well; I didn't thirst for education as Mary did. I'm slightly surprised that my father didn't press the matter, on principle, but he said he wouldn't have his daughters treated as second-class as they would have been at a school at which many of the pupils in those days were "private". Also — strangely, perhaps for one so hot on equality — he didn't feel easy about educating women.

Mary liked politics from an early age, and of course, leaned towards the left — not necessarily because these were our father's views; indeed, they argued quite hotly at times, and he quite enjoyed this until her arguments began to make more sense than his. Then, he got very red in the face and told her to be quiet, she was just a child and had a lot to learn. He didn't really want girls to be "clever". But he admired spirit, and she certainly had that.

His own spirit needed all the boosting it could get. For Dad and his like, the dole queue was a place of bitter humiliation, made, it seems, even more humiliating that it need have been, and as weeks stretched into hopeless months and then passed the year mark, a greyness seemed to settle on him. Although a rather gentle man, he had been raised in the tradition of the big, strong head-of-the-house who made all the important decisions and fed his family by the labour of his hands (he drew a veil over his own father's shortcomings in that respect). Without this manly image of himself, he crumbled. There was a time when he spoke of suicide — though of course Mary and I knew nothing of this. Somehow he still managed to drink, and this, rather than helping him to forget his troubles, made him more sharply aware of them.

This period of black despair came and went at intervals throughout our years at the cottage, and these were hard days for our mother, who had difficulties enough without the added strain of worrying about him. Self-pity disgusted her, and perhaps that was the best attitude she could have adopted; sympathy might have been fatal. Mostly, he did try to come to terms with his situation. He would set off on his bike and go round the building sites, land-clearing projects, anywhere where there might be a few week's work — or even a few days. Sometimes he was lucky — if it can be called lucky to dig ditches in knee-deep water in the middle of January. His wage for this was about what he would have got on the dole, but it helped his self-esteem for a little while. But he hated "navvying", hated the way the casual labour force was treated, "Like coolies," and he despised himself for having to do it.

But to be honest, it's hard to see what he was qualified for, for he had very little training, except in the use of a machine gun. I suppose in more prosperous days he might have made a passable clerk, except that writing was a strain for him, with his poor withered hand. Also, it must be said, he didn't come over as "respectable" enough for a white-collar job in those days, and the Bolshie reputation he was acquiring would hardly have endeared him to an employer. Perhaps a position as a minor Union official would have been the thing for him — but he was in the wrong part of the country for that. So he struggled on, doing a week or two's labouring when it presented itself — but that was quite rare, and remained so for nearly four years.

Once Mary and I went pea-picking with him after school. It was a dismal day of intermittent rain, yet the pickers worked on through it all, afraid that the overseer would tell them to pack up before they had earned what they needed. There were gypsies and children and tramps of both sexes — and my father and the other unemployed were indistinguishable from the tramps; they too wore old sacks over their heads to keep off the rain, and these had become saturated and heavy, and the ground was a quagmire. Everyone looked wretched and hopeless. The sky became more ominous, and the picking took on a desperate speed. When the downpour came, too blinding for even the hardiest to carry on, we took shelter under a tarpaulin-covered frame, and I can still remember the sick-making stench of unwashed bodies and wet hessian — and wretchedness, for that has a smell too. Then the overseer decided there would be no more work that day, and everyone lined up and he paid them, ten pence a sack. I had really only been playing about and eating more than I contributed, but Dad gave me threepence. Despite which I decided that I wasn't going to repeat the experiment. I felt . . . I can only describe it as "contaminated by hopelessness" and I think had only just begun to realise the depths to which our father had fallen.

One of my mother's tenets for life was, "It's a poor heart that never rejoices." I loved to hear her say this, because it meant that she was going to embark on a little extravagance for which she needed an excuse — for herself, if no one else. The most usual extravagance was a quarter-pound of Marie biscuits, and she treated herself to this sometimes on Mondays after a long day's washing, sending me up to the little shop, asking for them to be put on the bill till Saturday, while she set out the cups and boiled the kettle. Monday really was Washing Day, a whole day of it, for she had absolutely no conveniences — and in that she was much worse off than the Lucketts Lane ladies, notwithstanding their large families.

It has to be said in passing that the present-day obsession with personal cleanliness is a post-war development as far as the "poor" were concerned. The constant changing of clothes would have been impossible then; each member of the family would have perhaps one change of underclothes, and the changeover usually took place after the ritual Saturday night cleansing. My father normally had two clean shirts a week, unless a particularly dirty job upset the routine, but he would have three or four changes of collar in that time, lightly starched. Woollens would be worn many times without washing, as before the advent of synthetics they would simply have shrunk beyond recognition with frequent immersion, although they were washed with great care, if possible with rainwater from the butt. Almost everything apart from woollens and coloured were boiled and, as we had no copper, the boiling was done on the open fire in a big pan, the water of course being brought up in pails from the gate.

Each item would afterwards be tipped into the zinc bath and scrubbed on the corrugated washboard. We had no mangle, so everything, even blankets, had to be wrung by hand.

An unwritten law dictated that, come rain or shine, washing had to be done on Monday, "otherwise it hangs about all the week," so a dry windy Monday was a gift from the gods. The coming of efficient washing powders was regarded with suspicion: "they wear clothes out," and, "You can't get things clean without boiling. Stands to reason," no matter what the Rinso adverts said. Mary and I, students of the genre, in vain drew our mother's attention to the strip-picture story of the young wife always too tired to go out with her husband on Monday evenings to the detriment of their marriage (Out? On a Monday?). Then she discovered Rinso, after which her Monday evenings became a social orgy, and her husband fell in love with her all over again (Thinks: "thanks to Rinso!").

But Mum believed in Sunlight soap for all purposes, including hair and face washing. And she never wasted a drop of soapy water. When I arrived home from school I would find her scrubbing down the bit of concrete outside the back door with the leftover washing-water, reinforced with strong Jeyes Fluid, and she would have already washed the inside floors and the lavatories. No wonder she was ready for her cup of tea and her Marie biscuit. She would take off her apron, and we would sit in companionable silence, dunking our biscuits and reading our library books. After which respite there was the washing to be got in and folded for ironing — a long evening's work, that, with flatirons heated on the fire. And this, with darning and sheet-mending, was rather regarded as a relaxing evening chore (but not by our mother!).

I think it was Eleanor Rathbone, one of the stalwart Labour ladies of the period, who said that, "Sentiment placed a mother a little lower than the angels. Society put her a little higher than a serf." That was true of the working-class women of the 1930s, as true as it had been when my grandmother was raising her brood. I speak of country women, hamlet women — I think things had improved in the towns, where a working wife was not the exception. Admittedly, she was then doing two jobs instead of one, but there was the consolation of a bit of independence, and there were things to lighten her load denied to her rural sisters. The growing acceptance of birth control, for instance. Still a hole-in-the-corner business, at least in most towns information was available and becoming more so as the decade wore on. Surely that must have been the greatest of blessings in the days before Family Allowances and income support. A baby a year was by no means uncommon at the Tye, and it was no use the doctor saying (as he said to Mrs Trigg while she struggled from death's door after her sixth) that another would kill her. It was a rare doctor who would give contraceptive advice; a word to the husband was supposed to be enough. District nurses were discouraged from helping (a state of affairs which seems to have existed till the 1950s), and I don't think our splendid Nurse Peachey at the Tye was very well qualified in that department; there was nothing she didn't know about birth, people said, except what caused it.

My own curiosity was aroused when Mrs Tadgell was having her latest. I asked my father where she got them from, and he became very flustered and said the nurse brought them.

Did she have to pay?

"Yes."

Do they cost a lot?

"Yes."

Aha! thought I. Gotcha! For I knew quite well that a new baby was the last thing Mrs Tadgell wanted (Doris told me so). And in any case, how did it happen that the poorest people had the most babies?

I asked no further questions. I felt quite sorry for Dad, he was so unnerved. And from the agitated way my mother was dropping stitches in her knitting, I knew better than to take up the matter with her. (In fact, I never did.)

After the birth, a mother's first public appearance had to be at her Churching. In fact, I never saw some of the hamlet women at any other time. There were mothers who never appeared in public unless the back-garden washing-line could be called "public". The Lucketts Lane women like Mrs Trigg and Mrs Fowler were too worn out by child-bearing and rearing to have energy left for social life. Their Churching was their one moment of glory — if something conducted so sheepishly could be so described. I remember them coming into church at the end of Sunday School in their best coat and hat (the latter always seemed to be of dark brown felt and pulled well down). We whispered amongst ourselves while the older brothers and sisters of the new baby looked embarrassed as they hung around outside the church waiting for their mother. We knew there was something secret about the ceremony. I realise now that the occasion was treated as a ritual cleansing, a bit of real tribal magic, not, as surely it should have been, as a thanksgiving for a new life. Part of the ritual was the offering of a piece of silver. This problem was got over usually with a silver threepenny bit, a useful coin when sixpence would have been hard to spare. That accomplished, the woman could face the world again — and was probably in the running for another pregnancy before the year was out.

It occurs to me in passing that I never heard of a working-class mother at the Tye having a nervous breakdown. Presumably they were too physically worn out to realise they had "nerves".

As for interests outside the home, that seems to have been out of the question, and any "spare" time they had inside had to be usefully employed. There may have been women who actually enjoyed darning, but I never heard of them. (Imagine having seven sons to darn for, as my grandmother had, before the blessings of nylon!) I did once hear of a Tye housewife who liked embroidery — and that was considered by her peers to be a ridiculous waste of time and money, and an attempt to ape her "betters".

However, there were plans afoot to widen their horizons. The local gentry decided it was their duty to arrange this, and some ladies from the village-proper started up a Women's Afternoon once a week in the Mission Hall.

I must explain about the Mission Hall. It had been built, I judge, in the mid-Victorian era when the Established Church and its supporters were going through a burgeoning of righteous zeal, and worrying a good deal about the heathen in their midst. This is when the little church at the crossroads was built — a chapel of ease, I think it would be called — so that the erring flock from the two hamlets could no longer make the excuse that the walk to the village was too far for them. At the same time, the Mission Hall was an attempt to create a place for sober social intercourse and godly gatherings. It was hardly likely to empty the pubs. It was bare and Nonconformist in atmosphere, and smelled of mouldy hassocks as such places invariably did. There was a little stage, for speeches and talks and, in theory, the occasional concert, but in case it be thought that it could be used for ungodly entertainment, there was a large picture of Christ in Gethsemane presiding over it.

Nothing much happened there during our first year or two. The Sick Club met at intervals (and woe betide any man who was seen working his allotment when he was drawing money from it). Once there was a Whist Drive, an event giving rise to considerable excitement, and on one occasion the daughter of a well-heeled local farmer gave a birthday party there. We common children pressed our noses to the frosted glass, tantalised by the piano music and the blurred flitting figures as they passed within, and drooling at the eye-witness accounts of the cakes and jellies which had been carried in. Later, when we had a fairly young and vigorous new curate, the Reverend Garnet, he started a Young Men's Evening, when the local lads were invited to play darts and shove ha'penny and make fretwork letter-racks, hopefully to keep them out of the pub and away from the sins of the flesh. Later, the Reverend and Mrs Garnet held Missionary Evenings, at which we girls embroidered chair-backs and teapot cosies for sale, to raise money to support the propagation of the Gospel to our unenlightened brethren overseas, and we sang "From Greenland's icy mountains . . ." and had readings about Marys Slessor and Kingsley. Sometimes we had lantern slides, which was a tremendously thrilling and well-supported event, especially enjoyable when the slide appeared upside down and the Reverend G. lost his temper.

But at the time of its inception, the Women's Afternoon was something quite new for the Tye, and my mother, for one, quite enjoyed it. The invitation was for a "cup of tea and a chat" — but I imagine that such chat as there was must have been a bit stilted in the presence of the gentry. Still, it was a start, and sometimes there would be a guest speaker, and then there was a lady who had written a novel for which she had been unable to find a publisher, and she read instalments to her captive audience (which one suspects may have given her rather more pleasure than it gave them; but no matter, my mother for one thought it quite good, and, as an avid reader herself, her judgement had to be respected; she used to give us an update when we came home, for it was "a nice little story").

The good ladies who presided over these afternoons soon felt it their duty to widen their field of concern. Before long they were handing out wool for the knitting of squares for blankets — to send to the families of the unemployed in the North East! This raised Mum's hackles. For a start, the officiating ladies had much more time on their hands to knit squares than the hard-pressed local mothers, and for another, sympathetic though she was to any out-of-work family, she was irritated by the assumption — made by many, I gather — that "south of Watford Gap" unemployment and its attendant hardships were insignificant and somehow easier to bear. She said as much quite firmly, though she still accepted some wool and knitted a square or two half-heartedly. There was in her, with her upbringing and background, an inbuilt reluctance to "take on" the gentry; her tone in speaking to them was always "respectful" (I was often afraid that she might say "Ma'am" but she never did). Her views were discussed with some interest, and I don't think, in the end, much blanket-knitting got done; too many of the hamlet women agreed with her, though would never have said so in the presence of the presiding ladies.

There wasn't a lot of church-going at the Tye, and men never went at all, except, reluctantly, to christenings and funerals (not weddings, for the little church wasn't licensed). A few went to Harvest Festival, particularly if some of their own produce was on display, as Dad's was the year he had grown an enormous pumpkin, so big that we had to take it there in my old pushchair. He had been so proud of it, sure it would be given the place of honour. Alas, it was so big as to be an embarrassment, and finally was put to the back of the church at the foot of the old Tortoise stove (not yet lighted!) where it could hardly be seen. Dad was indignant, and I can't remember him ever voluntarily contributing again, though we were usually able to wheedle a few apples and dahlias if the frost hadn't got them. The smell of flowers and fruit and beeswax and oil lamps brings back to me a vision of the little church abnormally full, extra seats set up in the aisle to accommodate the sprinkling of men in their shiny serge suits, awkward until they lost themselves in belting out the old hymns: "We plough the fields and scatter" and "Come, ye thankful people, come!" when their voices swelled and boomed and their faces grew rosy with enjoyment. But mostly they just went along with the convention of sending their offspring to Sunday School, the ha'penny collection being a small price to pay for having the house and their wives to themselves for most of the afternoon. (A mixed blessing, I see now, for a woman who had literally "slaved over a hot stove" all morning and then washed up, and who might infinitely have preferred a quiet nap to an afternoon of "romance".)

Except when we had visitors, when all the rules went overboard, Sunday was a time of enforced good behaviour in our house. This was still fairly common, particularly where the mother, at least, remembered her

Victorian childhood (we realised, of course, that few rules applied to fathers).

Because we were in an unnatural state of cleanliness due to the ritual Saturday night ablutions, but also because it was apparently wicked to behave like children on the Sabbath, we were not allowed to climb trees, nor could we sew, knit, play cards, run through or round the house, shriek or do handstands on the green, whistle or sing. Hymns were allowed, and the Londonderry Air (for a long time I thought this was called the London Dairy Air); this, though not strictly speaking a hymn, must be all right because Mrs Blackwell played it on the harmonium at church. How all these taboos suddenly became non-taboo with the influx of summer visitors was a mystery, but we were careful not to rock the boat by asking questions.

One aspect of a country Sunday which must be mentioned was the Sunday evening walk. This was in summer, of course, weather permitting (and weather usually did permit in those childhood summers of blessed memory). After tea, and after a suitable period of rest for the grown-ups while we children kicked our heels and swung on the fence, my father would polish his boots and put a clean handkerchief in his top pocket, and Mum would wipe a powder puff over her cheeks and put on her hat and her thin summer coat, and Mary and I would be called in to have our faces washed and our hats put on, coats to be carried in case it got chilly, and we'd set off, Dad pausing to pick a buttonhole from his precious flowerbed.

He liked to walk a few paces in front, very erect on these occasions, his bowler hat very straight and firm, his walking stick swinging in the manner of a military swagger cane, his navy blue suit not looking too much as though it had belonged to somebody else, his watch chain giving no indication that it bore no watch. But I'm afraid he never did look quite as respectable as he thought, and as we children got older we used to hang back and giggle a bit. Once, a few years later, Mary dared me to creep up behind him and ram his hat over his ears and say "You are Mr Lobby Ludd" (a mystery man who figured in one of the newspaper publicity stunts). I did so. Dad was furious. His dignity was important to him — but only on certain occasions, and the early stages of the Sunday evening walk was one of them.

However briskly we set off, our walking soon became a stroll, and we would meet other families similarly attired, similarly strolling. It was a "respectable working-class" activity. The very poor (well, we were that, but we were different) and those over-blessed with children and under-blessed with an appreciation of life's finer things — they didn't take Sunday evening walks. The Tadgells, for instance — but then, neither did the Johnsons, but that was because Mrs Johnson thought walking in the country old fashioned, a view that was becoming more prevalent as the decade wore on. But we, on the whole, enjoyed them, which is perhaps strange when walking was an everyday necessity and rarely undertaken for pleasure. It was a very staid exercise, and our best straw hats hurt our ears, and we weren't allowed to scramble, but anything was better than the boredom of Sabbath evenings at home with nothing to look forward to but Monday morning and school.

Occasionally our progress was enlivened by meeting a courting couple, either walking sedately, arms linked, eyes demurely lowered, or sometimes sitting on a gate by a field, edging apart as we approached. They would respond mumblingly to our parents' greeting for they were usually young people we knew, then, when we were nearly out of earshot they would giggle, and if we looked back (reproached by Mother) they would be cuddling again, stirring my curiosity. Was this Love? What was so delightful about all that pushing and shoving? How long did it go on for? What would happen when we were out of sight? If Mary had any ideas on the subject, she never communicated them.

We were allowed to pick wild flowers so long as we didn't get dirty and it didn't involve scrambling. I delighted in making little posies for my father to wear in his buttonhole. Usually he had a pansy or two from the garden, and to these he would happily add "wild sweet peas" (tares), fingers and thumbs, dog daisies, and pink "plum puddings" — he would find room for whatever I picked for him, and wore them with pride, in the face of derision from his drinking mates when later he joined them in the pub. "What you wornt wearin' they owd weeds?" I once heard a voice from the taproom demand. They were never weeds to Dad; nor should they have been.

The main event on the national scene in 1935 was the Silver Jubilee. It is said that King George V expressed surprise at the enthusiasm with which the event was celebrated; he had no idea that he and the Queen were regarded with such affection. I think it was because they represented stability and sanity in an increasingly uneasy world. Dull they may have been, but no-one doubted their integrity and devotion to their "peoples". Also, people were hungry for something to feel happy about. There had been so much grey in their lives for so long.

One offshoot of the celebration was, for me, an enhanced appreciation of history. I had always had a feeling for it, and was fortunate in having at the time a teacher for whom the subject was a passion. With the cigarette companies bringing out a series of "Kings and Queens" picture cards, avidly collected, I began to see history as a panorama, each period fitting neatly into its appointed place, each with its own colour and ambience. That it was a picture-book version of history didn't matter. I was hooked.

My memories of the event are hazy. Heat — though early May — and drinking scalding hot tea in the Public Hall in the village, feeling that the cakes should have been more interesting on such a momentous occasion: large slabs of fruit and madeira cake didn't strike me as particularly festive. Afterwards we went to the park — disappointingly (to me) not a park in the municipal sense, but the parkland of the Great House wherein lived the squire and his lady wife who had vaguely royal connections (but with whom my mother had been to tea because she collected funds for the District Nurse, and Lady F. was the local patron). In the park there were races and competitions. I hated both. There were lots of flags about, and the aristocracy mingling with the peasants in a conspicuously democratic manner. To be fair, because the gentry in the village were (mostly) "the real thing" (and you couldn't deceive the real villagers) they could do this quite comfortably and without affectation. There was a greasy pole to be climbed, with a side of bacon at the top for the successful competitor. The sun blazed, making the grease even greasier.

"I sh'n care to eat that after thass bin in the sun all day," some bystander remarked.

In fact, there were no takers. Towards the end of the long afternoon some intrepid young man was persuaded by the Estate Manager, I think, to have a go, and stripped to the waist, dripping greasily like the pole itself, he struggled upwards to the accompaniment of ragged cheers. I can't remember whether he actually reached the top, but I fancy he was awarded the prize.

I recall the smell of hot, crushed grass, and a flat, tired feeling that Jubilees weren't really any big deal, and hardly worth waiting twenty-five years for.

The Jubilee celebrations were, in a way, our swan song at the Tye. At around that time, a pair of respectable artistic ladies had passed our cottage in their little car and had fallen in love with it. They found out who owned it and made Randall an offer of two hundred pounds for it, not even asking first to see inside. Of course, they were only interested if it was vacant . . .

Randall was tempted. Farming was in the doldrums, times were hard. He needed a tractor if he was going to make the farm a viable concern. He came to see my parents and asked what he should do. Of course, there was no need for him to do that: we had no security of tenure. But he was a friend as well as a landlord.

There were no other cottages available for us, and the Council houses were all heavily occupied, so we were in a difficult position, knowing how much two hundred pounds would make to Randall. He would never have dreamed of asking for that much; not everyone was prepared to pay over the odds for "quaintness", not in those days. The artistic ladies wouldn't wait forever.

What he came up with was the offer of a temporary home at the farm until something more suitable could be found.

As my parents saw it, they had no choice. They accepted.

CHAPTER
FIVE

A Growing Summer

Butlers Hall was a farmhouse of some antiquity, a fact
not much appreciated by its owners who only admitted
to its being "very old". Basically it was the typical
"hall" of mediaeval times, wattle and daub, heavily
beamed, with adjacent "usual offices", no doubt
previously called buttery, stillroom and so on, and
added to the main structure was a newer (i.e. Tudor)
"solar" gable, the downstairs of which was referred to
as "the two parlours", one of which was allocated for
our use, with bedrooms over the old "hall".

I don't remember moving. It was just a matter of
leaving for school from one house and going home at
the end of the day to another. I don't remember having
any regrets at leaving the Tye, and felt very little
strangeness, and indeed felt great pleasure in going into
the lovely old house through the side door which led
into a little dark hall, and then into what was to be our
living room, a very pleasant sunny room with windows
on two sides, one overlooking the orchard and the other
an enclosed garden (perhaps once a herb garden?) but
at that season — it was June — heady with the perfume
of lilies and roses, with subtle undertones of lavender

and fern, mint and box hedge just (mercifully) winning
the battle with the less agreeable odour from the nearby
privy, screened by a curtain of ivy. This was a two-holer,
as farm privies often were — and in fact, this one was a
two-and-a-half holer, for it had a lower seat as well for
younger members (what a convivial picture of family
togetherness that conjures up!).

Upstairs, Mary and I were to sleep in what had
probably been the farmhands' room, frugally lighted,
and beyond it was a large east-facing bedroom
allocated to my parents, which had a frieze of plaster
Tudor roses (quite famous, these roses, I later found,
for they are mentioned in, I think, the Victoria County
History). The Randalls knew nothing of these things,
and cared not at all.

Cooking facilities were non-existent, so Mum was
even worse off than before, having to make do with an
oil stove in the corner of the little hall where she could
only see to cook if the outside door was open (there
was, of course, no electricity and just a tap in the
farmyard). No sink, of course, no washing facilities, but
we coped — or, rather, Mum coped. I have no doubt
we bathed, somehow, but I have no recollection of it. It
must have been exhausting for Mum, but for us, the
compensations were enormous.

There is always one summer in childhood which we
remember as idyllic, and that, for me, was our summer
at Butlers. Day followed sunny day and I felt
extraordinarily happy. The animals didn't interest me
much. In the heat they smelled and were plagued with
bluebottles, and I avoided them, except when taken by

Randall to see a newborn calf, damp and curly from its mother, staggering on newborn legs. The great Shire horses were dear old things, huge and patient and gentle, but I was afraid of their big feet. Soon they would be made redundant by the new tractor. Tommy was a favourite of ours. He was the pony who pulled the milk cart, and often on a Saturday morning I would go out with Randall, he standing up in his chariot, I clinging on beside the gleaming milk churn from which he filled his customers' jugs. We rattled down the lanes in fine style, between hedges thick with wild roses; exhilarating it was. Sometimes I was allowed to take the reins; Tommy needed no bidding, he knew just when to stop, lingering longer than necessary at the houses where he got some little titbit. At the end of the round he would be set loose into the orchard, and would race off in a wild, whinnying gallop, revelling in his release, just as I did when I got in from school and ran into the orchard and did handstands.

Our London relations came as usual at the Bank Holiday. The Randalls didn't seem to mind and we crammed them in somehow. Mrs Randall was rather pleased, I think; her life was so dull, such a round of drudgery, as I suppose it was for all working farmers' wives, and she had seen so few people. I think she must have been under forty at that time, with thick dark hair she wore in a bun — she had a lot of trouble with the bun. And she sprayed her listeners as she talked. But she was quite nice, almost girlish sometimes, and cheerful. I don't think she had any idea of what went on beyond the end of the lane, and there were no neighbours for about half a mile. The family consisted of herself and her husband, and their son John, mentioned earlier; and there were her parents, an old country couple who really seemed like a leftover from another age, keeping themselves very much to themselves, and only slowly coming round to accepting us, after which Mum became a great favourite. I think they may have been the real owners of the farm, and Mrs R. (Amy) their only child who Randall had had the good sense to marry (like the Farmer's Boy in the old song — and what a good move it was, apparently for all concerned). Having us in the house did wonders for Amy, and like everyone else, she got very attached to my mother.

We had started going to the pictures about this time. Occasionally we had gone in the past, to the fairly new cinema in the town, and had been thrilled by the glamour of it, enhanced by our cigarette collection of "stars" like Myrna Loy and Clark Gable, and an occasional glimpse of magazines like *The Picturegoer*. That year, 1935, someone had thought it a good idea to build a "picture palace" — a proper one, none of this made-over village hall stuff — on the edge of a village no bigger than our own about five miles away. (In fact one of my father's casual labouring jobs the previous year had been at the site). The idea was, obviously, that film fans from the neighbouring villages would patronise it. The idea might have been a good one, but the little matter of transporting the would-be patrons had been overlooked. Within a few weeks, alarmed by the thin audiences, the cinema laid on a bus to tour the area, but the overall fare was a shilling, and added to the cost of a cinema seat (for most of us, in the sixpence to ninepence range) it made an expensive night out for a family. Car-owners (rare animals) obviously preferred the fleshpots of the town, where their cinema-going could be combined with other attractions.

We went by train. This was unsatisfactory, for the train service wasn't geared to the cinema timetable, with the consequence that we never saw a programme all through, and never the main feature. We went on the 5.30p.m. train from the village — and oh! the excitement of those summer evenings: walking down to the station through the fields, always afraid we might miss it, puffing and panting up the incline to the station — history now, of course; the dear little line was one of the first victims of the infamous Dr Beeching. The journey was about three miles, and cost sixpence, threepence for children — the same price as the cinema tickets. We would arrive halfway through the Big Picture so we knew the end before we knew the beginning. The audience would consist of half a row of sixpennies and rather less in the ninepennies. If people wanted to show off, they might treat themselves to the one and ninepennies, but they were rare. Once we actually saw a couple on the "balcony" — half a crown! — and figured that it was a young man in love with more money than sense.

The "B" picture was usually about singing cowboys or an American "sitcom" family called The Joneses. Then we had to sit through the adverts for the local hairdresser and the Orange Tea Rooms, then a documentary which always seemed to be about coal, a "Silly Symphony" (cartoon) which was especially enjoyed, then the Forthcoming Attractions (which made us mentally swear to come next week, come what might). And only then, with the clock in the corner of the auditorium moving inexorably towards 8.20p.m. when we would have to leave to catch our train, the Main Feature, of which we had already seen the end. Slowly and with many a backward glance we edged towards the exit, always hoping that we would come to the point at which we'd come in, but of course we never did, not once. Out into pale reality then, and a gallop to the station, for the train was the last of the day and the alternative was a roundabout five-mile walk, which surely would have dampened our cinema-going ardour. In this piecemeal way we saw some of the great film classics — and some better forgotten — Greta Garbo, Madeleine Carrol, Carole Lombard, Dick Powell, Gable, Conrad Veight (Boo!) and Shirley Temple, who I envied and hated and cried over when she did her Little Eva bit, Busby Berkley extravaganzas (how did they do it?), Will Hay, Laurel and Hardy (the Marx Brothers I was unable to appreciate). But we never saw what could be called a real love story, except sweet ones like "Smilin' Through" (over which we wept copiously). "Love", in the grown-up, mysterious sense, was denied to us — the Hays Office and our mother saw to that — and if, despite her vigilance, we found ourselves watching a scene which featured lovers not behaving as decorously as they should, she whispered

144

"Shut your eyes!"(We didn't — but I think she probably did.)

Mrs Amy Randall had never had the opportunity of being corrupted in this way. I don't think she had ever been to the pictures before we went to Butlers. My mother invited her to join us. Randall didn't mind, but her parents were dubious, for it meant we wouldn't be home before half past nine, and they shared my grandfather's opinion that "there was no good on the roads after nine o'clock".

I can't recall Mrs Randall ever commenting upon a film we had seen, but they must have been an eye opener to her. It's hard to imagine now how small her world was, without neighbours (surprisingly, they weren't even churchgoers). I never saw her with a book or newspaper. But they did, rather surprisingly, have a wireless, only switched on for the weather and fatstock prices. I never heard music, and only once remember it being used for sheer entertainment. It was a rare thing for any of them to sit in the front parlour, which I think was much as it had been since the old couple's marriage. There was a rosewood piano, never played; it had cost the incredible sum of one hundred pounds, Amy said, just after the war, so that may have been at the time of her wedding ("things were very dear then"). The cost must be multiplied many times to compare it with modern values. That the Randalls (or the parents) had let their hair down to the extent of buying something so frivolous — and costly — as a piano threw a new light on the household.

145

I remember Amy and my mother sitting in the parlour on a summer evening; the outer door was open and I sat on the front step. The wireless was switched on at eight o'clock and we listened to "Music Hall". The top of the bill was probably the Western Brothers ("Good evening, cads!") or Elsie and Doris Walters, the "loveable" Cockney sisters. After "Music Hall" was finished, the set was left switched on — or it may have been on another occasion about that time; I sat in the lovely summer dusk and we heard the voice of Adolph Hitler addressing one of his rallies (could it have been the famous Nuremberg one?). I don't know whether it was "live" or recorded, but I do know it chilled me. Up until then, although we had heard of Hitler, he had been a sort of joke, with his strutting and his Chaplin moustache. Now, hearing that harsh, ranting voice, belligerent and hate-filled, being greeted with roars of Teutonic adulation, it was as though the bogeyman which had haunted all my young life had risen up and was shaking its fist at me. We didn't need a translation of the words; it was a language anyone could understand. My heart sank as I saw my mother's grave face and heard her say to Amy "surely we're not going to have to go through all that again . . ." Just as the cloud of the first Great War had hovered over my earlier childhood, so the shadow of the second was creeping towards me in the run-up to adolescence.

But . . . it was easy to push such thoughts to the back of my mind in those sunlit days at Butlers. The farm was in the throes of harvest, and there were golden days when, in theory, we were helping in the fields, but I can only remember lying on my back on top of a swaying, loaded wagon, the sky blue and cloudless above me, while the patient horses plodded up the slope to the farmyard. (How thoughtless of me to add to their burden!) For them, there wouldn't be many more harvests, not with the new tractor already ordered. This was my real growing summer, that interlude between childhood and puberty which changes us from the cute child to the gangling and bewildered teenager (another of those words which weren't going to be in common usage for another nine or ten years). Perhaps mine was the last generation before "the awkward age" (which had to be got through as quickly as possible) became the period during which all of fashion, and music, and entertainment, and "style" were geared to making it the most (theoretically) enjoyable of one's life.

Mary's metamorphosis was more striking than mine. She was fourteen and had left school in July, and suddenly she was on the other side of the great divide. She was now considered a young woman in that it was time for her to earn her own living. There was no careers advice at school for the likes of us. When the date of our leaving approached we had to write down on a piece of paper what we wanted to do. Mary would have liked to put "Secret Service" because she had fancied that ever since reading the stories in our penny Sunday comic (*The Joker*) a few years earlier. Since she was now of an age to realise that any vacancies in that profession were rarely available to fourteen-year-olds who hadn't been to Grammar school, she thought "Civil Service" had a promising ring to it. But a sudden rush of modesty and realism made her put what other girls of her background were putting: she wrote "Domestic Service" — with a sinking heart, I'm sure, realising that in doing so she was putting herself in a slot from which she might never escape. At least there were always vacancies there. The ladies of the village were tireless in their search for girls to "train in their ways", to replace those ungrateful young women who, having been so trained, then shed their caps and aprons and headed for the fleshpots of the town factories or Woolworth's, or married the grocer's boy. These would-be employers descended like locusts on the school towards the end of term; the more aristocratic just let it be known that they were interested.

Mary was invited to an interview at the Rectory, where Lady Phyllida was looking for a kitchen maid (for this was a very high-class incumbency). My mother went with her. She knew Lady Phyl — we all did; she was a well-known local figure, mildly eccentric but also quite practical, and completely unaffected — that is an understatement. Sartorially, she didn't give a damn. She was rarely seen without an old brown beret on her head, and wore tweeds which must have been good once, somewhere around 1920. She wore darned lisle stockings and sensible shoes, and her greying hair was never quite under control. She was respectful to my mother, who in recognition called her "my lady".

Because creature comforts meant nothing to her personally, Lady Phyl didn't give her servants' comfort a very high rating in her list of priorities. Because she was unstinting in her own service to "good causes", she expected the same unstinting devotion from her staff to her family. Nonetheless, she was compassionate in times of trouble and brought up (like Mrs Musgrave) with a strong sense of noblesse oblige. Mum knew and felt safe with the type, and since Mary seemed happy enough with the situation, it was agreed that she should start work at a wage of twenty pounds a year, all found except for clothing. In working hours (which was nearly all the time) her uniform was to consist of two morning dresses of light blue cotton, two darker afternoon ones, caps and aprons to go with them, and dark stockings and shoes. There would be one afternoon off a week, to start when the lunch things were washed up, and alternate Sunday mornings and afternoons, plus one weekend a month (though that was in theory; sometimes she had to forego this). Her day would start at 6.30a.m., when she would rake the fires and take the cook a cup of tea. From then it was all go until lunch, after which she would be "off duty" till she had to get afternoon tea, i.e. the most free time would be of two hours' duration, and even this would be filled with "relaxing" little jobs like sheet-patching — which was no relaxation for Mary! At the end of the day, with the dinner things washed up and the kitchen cleared and set out for the morning, the rest of the day was her own! But as it would be about ten o'clock by then, it would be as much as she could do to climb the dark wooden stair (a veritable death trap in the event of a fire) to the unheated attic room under the eaves which she would share with Kathleen, the house-parlourmaid.

Strangely, she didn't flinch from all this. The uniform was bought from the draper's in the High Street, and she was ready. And never, in the months to come, did I once hear her grumble.

Much was changing in our relationship. We were entering a new era. My whole life had been spent in Mary's shadow, and I had felt her love and protection around me through most of childhood's ups and downs. Now, at the age of fourteen-and-a-quarter, she was a woman, with already a woman's shape, with her adult life starting, leaving me behind, a child still. But not so much a child as I was.

It was lonely at the farm without her (for John Randall was busy helping his father, and in any case we had very little in common). But I had friends, and in the last two or three weeks at the farm life was pleasant, even with the dread of the new school year looming. One friend (though never a really close one, for she was thirteen) was Lucy Fardell who lived near the little church, and she would come and we would make a little house in a disused chicken shed. Lucy was good at little houses, but not very imaginative. She was the object of much interest because her mother had died, which seemed to me (and of course was) the greatest tragedy that could befall a child. Lucy was the youngest of a large family, mostly boys, and on the mother's death her only sister had been brought home from service to do her duty, that is, assume the rôle of "mother" to a family consisting of five brothers and Lucy, plus her father. She did this without question. She had a young man, who lived two doors away, very quiet and respectable and an only son. They seemed happy and well-suited and looked likely to have a long and tranquil marriage, but he developed pneumonia. The word had a terribly sombre ring to it in those days — it would be about five years before a medical breakthrough would reduce its terrors; but that was too late for John. I remember one of our tradesmen telling my mother with gloomy relish that "the crisis was expected tonight". How dreadful for his poor mother to watch the hours ticking away as he deteriorated, praying that the crisis would pass and leave him "sleeping natural", like Beth in *Little Women*. But no such luck for John. Maggie wore a black armband for a long time, but eventually married someone else, and absorbed him into the household. But by that time some of the brothers had married also, and Lucy was in service.

Towards the end of our Tye days Mum had got herself a cleaning job, tipped off by the postman: "They want someone a bit special and I thought of you." The people were a Mr Britnell and Miss Harker, and they had bought the Smiths' old house at the Green. Theirs was, for those days, a very unusual partnership, a platonic one (no-one seems seriously to have doubted this, including my mother); in any case, they had a chaperone in the shape of Miss Harker's mother who had had a stroke, and had probably put up some of the money. Her late husband had been in the Royal Flying Corps, and although he survived the war (unusual for airmen) he had died a year or two later. It had been established beyond reasonable doubt that his injuries, or the ill health from which he died, had been the result of his wartime experience, yet his widow had been awarded no pension. For years she had fought, needing the money to bring up her four children and educate them suitably, finally taking her case to the House of Lords, where at last she had been rewarded, not only with a pension but with the outstanding backlog, and this, no doubt, had gone towards the purchase of Pigotts.

But her battles had all but finished her, health-wise, and she needed support, hence the idea of a home in the country with her daughter and friend. They were not at all well-off, however, and time would prove that they had bitten off more than they could chew, but in the early days, everything looked rosy, the house on the Green being a fulfilment of many a suburban dream. My mother went to "do" for them, and although the money was only about sixpence an hour, it was the beginning of an upturn in our fortunes, making more frequent the occasions for the heart to rejoice, and Mum became much more than the daily treasure to them. (She became such a friend, indeed, that the connection only completely ended on Mr Britnell's death more than fifty years later.)

One day when she was cleaning he came to her, rosy with euphoria, and said, "Mrs R., congratulate me! I've asked Miss Harker to marry me and she has consented!" and he gave her a kiss. Mum was just astonished that the consent had apparently taken him quite by surprise. Miss Harker herself was quite blasé when Mum offered her good wishes. She was quite a tough lady, for all her apparent fragility. The marriage took place without any fuss, in a registry office, the bride wearing her sister's fur coat, and she had chosen one of the new platinum rings — "Like a bit of old tin," said Mum. "Not like a wedding ring at all."

Women, especially middle-class women, didn't work after marriage (in many professions they weren't allowed to). Mrs Britnell fancied running a little village store, and to this end had the end of the old stable block converted for the purpose. For a time, earlier, Mary had worked there on Saturdays, for a shilling, which may sound like slave labour but the shop wasn't making any money (it's doubtful whether its proprietor could have run a jumble stall), and anyway, Mary enjoyed it and would have cheerfully worked for nothing. By this time we were almost considered part of the family, and when Mr Britnell was offered a job up North and was faced with the prospect of moving (hopefully leaving his mother-in-law behind) he asked if we would like to move into Pigotts, to our mutual advantage — that is, we would pay a nominal rent, which would help with the mortgage and give us a roof over our head, and Mum would keep an eye on Mrs Harker and do a bit of cleaning, while Dad kept a general eye on the property and did what he liked with the (very large) garden.

It solved our problem as well as theirs, and our summer idyll at Butlers came to an end.

CHAPTER
SIX

Pigotts

The men who built Butlers Hall almost certainly built Pigotts, for the plan was the same, except that the gable bit was smaller. It had stopped being a farm many years earlier, but there was still a dairy (a useful place to put things; my family were always great collectors of "things") and a brewhouse with a huge fireplace and a copper that was lined with real copper, probably as old as the house. Outside this was a little L-shaped courtyard with cobblestones and white fantails, and an old sink covering the spot where the well had been.

When we told our hosts at Butlers of our intended move, the old lady had said to Mum: "Oh, I wouldn't spend a night in that house! Not for a hundred pounds I wouldn't!" For it was said to be haunted, a fact my mother kept from me, but I was soon enlightened by my schoolmates. There had been a murder, they said, a nasty messy business, on the turret stair leading up to the attic: "And they've never got the bloodstains out, no matter how hard they've scrubbed!" I went to investigate, with some trepidation, but the stairs had been heavily varnished, so I didn't know what conclusion to draw from that. In passing I should add that at the Tye, belief in ghosts was shared by many of the older residents, and among the Lucketts Lane fraternity there were those who wouldn't pass a certain barn after dark for fear of seeing things that should not be seen. I have to say that although I had some very uneasy moments at Pigotts, particularly when I slept once in the attic bedroom, nothing happened that couldn't be explained away by my being blessed (?) with a colourful imagination. I missed Mary terribly at nights.

During our absence from the Green, there had been several comings and goings. The birds of passage of our earlier days had left. Most of the children had gone — and there had never been many.

Old Mr Smith had sold our previous home after a short residence in it, and built himself a four-square house of almost criminal ugliness next to Pigotts. In our old home were now installed the Campbells. The parent Campbells were in late middle age, very respectable. Mr Campbell didn't go out much; Mrs C. was small and lively, an unlikely mother for Miss Louie, whom we rarely saw. I think she had been born "late in life", and it showed. An only child and naturally retiring, she was also a semi-invalid — a self-induced invalidity, local opinion had it, encouraged by her parents, no doubt out of a desire to protect. I remember Mrs Campbell saying, quite proudly, that when Louie was a child she never wanted to go out and play; she'd say: "must I, Mamma? I'd rather stay here with you and do my sewing." Poor Louie. Within two or three years her father was dead, and she took to her bed, helping to eke out the family income by knitting to order, which she did exquisitely, while her mother ran up and down administering to her, wearing herself to a shadow.

At the adjoining house, wherein had lived the Browns/Edwards/Cochranes, there now lived two maiden ladies of uncertain age who supplemented whatever income they had by a bit of dressmaking and selling bric-à-brac and little embroidered trifles. (I bought a bit of china from them once, for my mother.) Later, when one of the ladies had to go into hospital, my mother offered my companionable services to the other, to sleep there at nights. I'm sure I went under protest, but the little lady fussed over me and made me very comfortable, perhaps quite enjoying having someone to "mother". The bleakness of their lives made me resolve not to be an old maid if I could help it. There were so many of them at that time, women who would have been wives and mothers had it not been for the awful slaughter of the war, and often their situation was pitiful.

When they moved on, they were replaced by the Gilroys. He was a Scot with a sandy moustache and something a bit shifty about him, I thought. I think he was a commercial traveller. His wife was sweet, neat and nicely spoken. Unfortunately, she had been scarred quite badly from a burn. They became friendly with my mother, and I have a sneaky feeling that Mr G. found Mum more attractive than he should. Not that that would have cut any ice with my mother, though she wasn't above appreciating the boost to her morale. I don't think they were childless by choice. They took me out once or twice in their car, and although car ownership was still pretty unusual in our circle, it was more common than it had been earlier in the decade.

The little shop had, of course, changed hands with the Britnells' departure. The new proprietor, the wife of the landlord of one of the village pubs, was a Londoner, with frizzy, too-black hair and jangling earrings. I don't think trade had improved a lot, and she moaned often to my mother about the locals, who probably were aware that she despised them as "yokels". She poured out her troubles to Mum, making it clear that she regarded her as a fellow ex-patriot, a cut above her rural neighbours: "You know what country people are like . . ." Indeed Mum did, being one herself, which Mrs Jones didn't seem to realise. Mum hadn't much time for her; I always knew the signs, from the set of her lips, but Mrs J. took her restrained response to indicate agreement.

On the east side of the green were three old cottages. In the first, an unattractive, tar-washed place, there lived a crusty old bachelor. My father called him Taffy, which the old chap resented bitterly, having been born in Monmouth. There was a vast and ancient yew tree at his gate. One Christmas Eve my Dad, returning from the pub with a few cronies, decided to give "Taffy" a Christmas surprise. He proceeded to decorate the tree with coloured party streamers which he just happened to have about his person. I was in bed and asleep so didn't personally witness this event, but shared Taffy's surprise on Christmas morning when daylight revealed the tree in all its festive glory. Taffy was incensed and muttered darkly that he "know'd the bugger what done it". But I like to think it gave him a little tingle of pleasure for his lonely Christmas. Long afterwards, the tattered remains clung to the old tree through winter frosts, February rains and March winds, and a few shreds still hung there when Spring brought the first of the London relations, giving Dad a fresh excuse for telling the tale, with a few embellishments.

Strangely, "love children" were rare, both at the Tye and on the Green. At the former, there was a very nice, cheerful young man, Tom something, who was the son of a respectable and respected lady we knew as Miss Dinah. There was no chip on Tom's shoulder, and no reason for one. He had no (known) father. From his age, one wonders if he was the result of a sad wartime liaison — perhaps the lover was a fiancé killed before a wedding could be arranged. Apart from Tom and a few christenings rather quickly following the weddings, the only other instance of an "illegitimacy" was that of Dorothy Day. Her mother, Ellen, had recently married one of the Fardell boys, thus uniting two of the older Council cottage families. Ellen was one of a large family of girls and, although single and still under thirty, was the mother of Dorothy, who was my age. Dorothy was a titian-haired, rather refined girl, quite unlike the Days. Once, when questioned, she said without embarrassment that her mother had thought her father would marry her but he'd gone away. We children were all interested in the Day/Fardell marriage because the bride wore blue. It was explained to me by my more worldly-wise acquaintances that this was because she wasn't "pure". I realised that this had something to do with the existence of Dorothy, but couldn't work out how.

Ellen always kept herself to herself, and had a rather hard, unsmiling face, but I can understand that; in a community like the two greens she must have felt herself constantly the object of pity and censure, and her hard shell must have grown out of a lot of pain. She was a good mother, in her undemonstrative way, and a hard worker. That she continued to support Dorothy without help from her new husband was revealed to us by the garrulous Mr Walters, from whom Ellen bought Dorothy's clothes. Such items were never ordered while her husband was around, and anything in the way of a little "extra" for Dorothy had to be arranged on the q.t. Nevertheless, the community seemed to feel that Ellen had been very lucky to get herself a decent chap like Len Fardell, and that she ought to be grateful.

On the home front, the economic climate was improving. With Mary away, there was one less mouth to feed and, best of all, Dad had at last landed himself a more-or-less proper job, the first for nearly five years. This was with a small building firm in the town five miles away. They wanted a painter and decorator and didn't want to pay much, so they accepted my father, inexperienced though he was. He was to receive a wage of tenpence an hour, as a "learner", under the head painter. It was really like being an apprentice, and the money was in proportion. Dad didn't complain. His take-home pay was about two pounds a week, less in

159

winter when daylight was short ("Heaven help the painter when the leaves begin to fall" was a favourite quotation of his; I think he may have got it out of his Socialist "bible", *The Ragged Trousered Philanthropists*, which he kept beside his bed until he died). But he had got back his self-respect, which was good to see.

He really worked hard at becoming a good painter. I don't know if he succeeded, as apart from his lack of flair for anything practical, he had the disadvantage of his poor withered right hand, but I do know he was a happier man, and had a good relationship with his fellow painter for the next four or five years ("me and Bert" became something of a family joke). He still drank as much as he could, often more than he could afford, but never in working hours. Had he done so, he would soon have got his cards. His boss, "Freddie" Palliser, was a god-fearing total abstainer, and would have considered it his Christian duty to take a firm line with any sinner. When a year or two later Dad felt confident enough to approach him for a rise, he clucked a good deal and looked gravely disturbed. He conceded at last that he might just see his way to increase the hourly rate by a ha'penny, emphasising that this generosity would cause him some difficulty and was in no way to be seen as a precedent. Despite this, Dad seemed to have a grudging affection for "Freddie", which is strange, for he had little time for bosses, particularly "Christian" ones.

As a tradesman, Freddie's standards were high, and his customers got value for money. He would drop in on his workmen at any time, and nothing slipshod escaped his eye. He hummed to himself as he went round. Sometimes his comments took the form of homemade lyrics to well-known hymns, and his pleasure or displeasure could be gauged by the liveliness or gloom of the hymn chosen. "Rock of Ages" in its drearier setting was a very bad sign.

Ours was a church school, which meant, among other things, that once past the Infants our first lesson — forty-five minutes of it — was Religious Instruction. We started each day with a prayer and a hymn and a short moral address from the teacher or Headmaster. Each day had its own hymn, and sadly one or two of the great stirring ones became quite unbearable to me because they came at the start of a day I particularly disliked. Above all, I hated Wednesdays, and only in old age have I begun to be able to appreciate the powerful beauty of "O Worship the King" which preceded the Wednesday programme. I hated Wednesdays because of Mrs L. (even now, I can hardly bring myself to speak her name). She was the Head's wife, not trained as a teacher at all; she had been a dressmaker. Needlecraft was her passion, and we were always being told by the Head that we were incredibly lucky to have the services (unpaid, I gather) of such a specialist. On reflection, I think I've met just three really cruel women in my life, and in putting Mrs L. at the head of the list I'm probably being unfair. I see now that she was a woman with problems. She was almost certainly in the throes of her mid-life crisis, and, surrounded as she was by children (for she lived on the school premises), every school day must have reminded her of her own childlessness. I would suspect that she hated children, but if she'd had them, they would have had to be girls — pretty, dainty little girls with well-controlled curls and clean fingernails who would have been good at needlework. That was her criterion. And I of course (and Mary before me) was hopeless. She had it in for me from the outset. Once she discovered that I had lost my thimble. This had been a source of much worry to me, and I didn't feel I could ask my mother for sixpence to get another at the draper's in the High Street. My sin was discovered, most publicly, in the presence of the Lady Inspector who was making an unannounced visit. I was hauled in front of the class and given the sort of interrogation that wouldn't have been out of place in the French Revolution. I shook dreadfully, as I always did in Mrs L.'s presence ("Stop shaking or you'll get a slap!" she used to say, at which of course I shook all the more). I remember the Lady Inspector looking at me kindly and saying, "I'm sure she'll be more careful in future." Mrs L. glared, and when the lady had gone, she simply couldn't let the matter rest. She kept on about it for days. And I was slapped. Not by Mrs L. herself, of course — she was too mindful of her position for that. But she deputed the task to my class teacher. She, elderly and overweight, performed uneasily but with a heavy hand, going very red with the exertion and with much wobbling flesh. But she wouldn't meet my eye and didn't enjoy it, for I think she rather liked me because I was rather good at the subjects she herself preferred. Painful though the punishment was, it was nothing to the pain of facing the school playground afterwards, aware of the embarrassed avoidance of my friends and the smug delight of my enemies, of whom the chief was Mrs L's own favourite, a pretty girl called Olive who had curls and sewed beautifully. My whole life at this time was overshadowed by Mrs L. She really knew nothing at all about children, particularly children who didn't conform, and I seem to have been labelled from my earliest schooldays as a nonconformist. And she didn't like girls who didn't shine at maidenly pursuits. But then, in those days, in schools like ours, it was made plain to us that girls were destined for one sort of life and boys for another, and woe betide children of either sex who had other ideas.

For instance, we had two annual prizes of fifteen shillings each, considered very generous, awarded by our School Governor, who was the Squire and a very well-connected person, for the village was unbelievably feudal. The prize for boys was for the pupil who came top in Arithmetic, and for girls the one who was considered best at Needlework. One amazing year it was I who came top in Arithmetic — quite untypically; the previous year I had been nearly at the bottom. Needless to say, the prize was awarded to the boy who came closest. Strangely, I didn't feel particularly sore about this — although my class teacher did — for I realised my score was untypical. But this is where the story gets incredible. Before I left that school, I discovered that I had one asset in the needlework field: I could embroider. I was called upon to embellish a winceyette nightdress of quite outstanding awfulness

163

over which I had laboured. Suddenly, holding a needle became a pleasure instead of a pain. The finished garment was almost pretty. And at the end of that school year, the unbelievable happened: I won first prize! (I can only assume Mrs L. wasn't among the judges.) It would be nice to be able to report that this was the beginning of a new era for me, but alas! my talents stopped there.

In general, I suppose our basic education was quite good, and with at least one teacher our English lessons instilled a love of poetry which has never left me. I remember how suddenly Keats' "Ode to Autumn" hit me with its beauty, fixed in my mind with a memory of the September sun shining through the window upon Michaelmas daisies and Miss Todd's auburn hair. History, as I have said, was a joy then and thereafter, though our studies ended with Queen Victoria. I suppose the powers that were had decided that later events might prove too unsettling for young minds. Geography was sweeping in its generalisations, but I joined in the patriotic pleasure of seeing all that red on the world map, and accepted without question that it was a Good Thing, and on Empire Day (when we had a half-day holiday) I wore my daisy with pride.

But these were lessons we shared with the boys. To return to the exclusively feminine arts, I suppose that with all this emphasis on sewing (which included instruction in every form of patching and darning) and on Cookery and Housewifery — subjects which were taught in the way our grandmothers might have been, making use of the cheapest cuts of meat and the most

164

basic materials, such as bath brick and even woodash for cleaning sinks — with all this, I say, we were being prepared for the lifetime of domestic drudgery which would presumably be our lot, one way or another. So, as future wives and mothers, it's strange that we were in no way prepared for what wife- and motherhood actually involved. Sex education in elementary schools was a long way off. I never once heard the word "sex" mentioned. Biology would have been considered an equally dirty word, I think. We did have a lesson called Hygiene, but that was about sleeping with our windows open and how good it was for us to have to walk three — indeed, six — miles a day to school. I can't remember that we were even told about washing our hands after going to the lavatory; perhaps the teacher felt that the word "lavatory" was taking us into dangerous territory.

We older children rarely had P.E., though we had "drill" perhaps once a week. That is, the Head would turn us out into the playground and tell us to run round it, then to stand still and swing our arms for a very long time. Sometimes he would disappear while this was going on, and then he'd come back and take out his watch and declare the session at an end. I think his object was to wear us out so that we had no energy left for being unruly. Not that we ever were. Discipline wasn't a problem, not with his frayed cane ever at the ready beside his desk.

I became a Girl Guide. I had been a Brownie, and enjoyed that. Our Brown Owl had been, at first, the Nannie from the Rectory — a very refined young lady

— and then when she left to marry the local grocer, we had the daughter of one of the big houses, a youngish, smart lady with time on her hands. An early recollection is of my going up the drive to the great door of The Hall, pulling the bell and, when it was answered by the butler (a rather grand personage), I produced a bit of paper with my hat size on it (for thus I had been instructed by Brown Owl), at which he solemnly produced a silver salver and said he would see that Miss Cicely received it.

When Miss Cicely married a year or two after this, Guides and Brownies formed a Guard of Honour, and there was a Wedding Breakfast laid on for the villagers in the Public Hall, and I had sip of champagne which I found very disappointing. The bridal pair mingled democratically and laughed a lot. (Much disapproval was expressed in the village because the bridegroom was Miss Cicely's cousin. The general opinion was (a) that she was getting on a bit and he was the only man who wanted her and (b) that it was a plot to keep all the money in the family. Actually, she was about thirty I should think, and very attractive.) They went abroad to live — in Kenya — and I can well imagine that they became part of the notorious "Happy Valley" set.

By the time I joined the Guides, the Guider was a Mrs Connell, one of those people one neither likes nor dislikes. She had two pretty daughters, an upper-middle-class manner, and seemed efficient and suitable, but wore the air of having something on her mind. What she had on her mind, it transpired, was the invisible Mr Connell, who, it was rumoured, had Strayed (whatever that meant). Such things as divorce were never mentioned in front of children, but somehow we got to hear of it, and found it very interesting. (Divorce, it went without saying, was something that only happened to the upper classes.) The fact that Mrs Connell was the innocent party didn't matter; it was unthinkable, apparently, for her to be in charge of other people's daughters. I suppose those were the Guide rules. At all events she did the honourable thing and resigned. I never heard her name mentioned again, or saw her or the girls. Being "a sister to every other Guide" apparently didn't apply if you had been involved, no matter how innocently, in divorce.

Guides was a great leveller. In my patrol we had a doctor's daughter, a Rector's, the daughter of an M.P. (who later blotted his copybook by meeting Hitler) and an Honourable (this last was a wild, scatty girl with a rich vocabulary). I don't think we were conscious of the social differences till later.

The next "proper" Guide Captain we had was Miss Sawyer, the sister of the new curate (Mr Garnet having been promoted and moved on). They lived in a small villa near the tuck shop, and seemed rather poor. Miss Sawyer was little and vivacious, more like a schoolgirl, and we liked her immensely. Mr S. was a bit of a wimp (a word then unknown) but he was nice, though perhaps not very impressive as an inheritor of the fiery Rev. Garnet's flock. Mr Sawyer was younger, and handsome, in a softer, almost apologetic way; and he was a bit naïf. An unmarried curate was a gift to the ladies, and it wasn't long before he fell victim. But before succumbing there were minor skirmishes, and the outcome of the saddest of these was that he drove poor Dorrie Fletcher into an asylum for love of him. Dorrie was a single lady in her late thirties. She lived with her elderly parents who had a smallholding near the little hamlet church, of which she had been an acolyte for some time, and had been my Sunday School teacher, perplexing me on many biblical matters which had previously seemed fairly straightforward; and she made and sold crocheted goods to raise money to assist the propagation of the gospel. She had seemed a nice, reasonably intelligent body, but sadly afflicted with a large goitre, and had very little else to mark her as different from the thousands of other excellent women of her kind. She didn't go to work, and had no social life except that offered by the church. Into this barren landscape had come nice Mr Sawyer, combining all the qualities of which poor Dorrie must have dreamed. His naturally kind heart and simple unworldliness allowed the situation to get out of hand before he realised what was happening. Before long, she was announcing their engagement. On a wave of euphoria, she became maniacally religious. The climax came when she was discovered up a ladder cleaning the church windows at four o'clock in the morning. They took her away after that. Perhaps she went on cherishing her illusions until she died. One rather hopes so.

Because Mr Sawyer realised now that he was a hunted man, he took refuge in the solicitous attentions of Miss Laura Mold, and when she, in quite a short space of time, also announced that they were engaged, he gave in gracefully. And in doing so, one is tempted to suspect that he may not have been quite as unworldly as he appeared. The Misses Mold were two ladies around forty who lived in a charming Queen Anne house in the High Street. Their father, a solicitor, had obviously left them well-provided for, and it seems strange that some fortune-hunting young man hadn't set his sights on one or other of them before this. Miss Jane was quieter and nicer, Miss Laura more vivacious, rather overpowering. Laura was interested in the Guides, which I suppose brought her a common interest with the Sawyers (it goes without saying that she was involved in most other church and village affairs). She once took us Guides for choral practice and accompanied us to Wembley to a big rally. She sat beside me and showed off by singing "Land of my fathers . . ." in Welsh, with embarrassing gusto. I suppose, really, such a zest for living was rather endearing. And she had a hide like a rhino. When she decided she was going to marry Mr Sawyer, he didn't stand a chance. The announcement of the betrothal came quite quickly, and after that she stuck like glue. I had left the village before the wedding so didn't see it (the Guides had been invited to be a Guard of Honour), and I heard later that the union was blessed with a daughter within the year; somehow people found that surprising. I believe the marriage was quite happy, although one thing they didn't have in common was a love of music; Miss Laura loved to sing, and sang well (and loudly), while Mr S. was tone deaf, and his chanting of the required pieces of the liturgy in church was the source of much merriment.

The first event I remember of 1936 was the death of King George V. The announcement that "the King's life is drawing peacefully to its close" is so Victorian — but of course, the King and Queen were real Victorians, as were my own parents, having been born in the old century. I went into my mother's bedroom that January morning as I always did, and she told me the news. I burst into tears and said, "But I never saw him!" He had been a remote, patriarchal figure, and I couldn't feel any sense of personal loss, but the feeling that an era had ended saddened me. "Four score years and ten, like the Bible says!" mumbled Mrs Harker. The thought seemed to give her a gloomy satisfaction.

The new King wasn't much more real to us than his father had been, and there followed nearly a year in which his activities were given only a selective publicity; nevertheless, it must have been dawning on royalty watchers for some time that he was more icing than cake, and that the icing itself was of dubious quality. But he had been the world's Prince Charming for so long that ordinary people, especially the young, went on believing in him, and rejoiced that, in some way, his accession was going to blow away the cobwebs and open the door to a bright new England, as uncluttered with Victoriana in outlook as our homes were becoming in decor.

Limited though we were in our perception of the world in those pre-television days, we were avid newspaper readers and of course, saw the newsreels at the pictures and occasionally had a chance to "listen in" on someone's wireless.

The *Queen Mary* embarked on her maiden voyage in the May. She had been launched the year before and we had been allowed to listen from the outside "cloister" at school to Mrs L.'s wireless. Although there was too much crackling to hear much of what was said (I presume the broadcast was "live"), the sense of occasion got through to me. Later, in the autumn of that year, that monument to past grandeur, the Crystal Palace, was burned down. My maternal grandmother had sung there in a choir as a child, about the same time as she and her schoolmates were rolling bandages for the wounded of the Franco-Prussian war, so perhaps it was a charity concert. And now it was gone. We stood in the garden at Pigotts and on the distant horizon we could see a faint glow like early dawn. Whether that was the Crystal Palace is debatable, but when we heard the news, that's what we believed.

Somehow it seemed terribly significant, as so many things did that year. October saw the great Jarrow March. There had been demonstrations and marches throughout the 1930s, and they were naturally given much space in the publications which came into our house. Although the Jarrow one was a "failure", in the sense of making an impression on the government of the day (and must have seemed so to the participants as they trailed back home in spiritless misery), it was a success in publicity terms. The home truths about the lives of the working classes (or, rather, the non-working) at last began to register with the middle- and upper-class Englishman in the relatively prosperous south (though my parents would have given a hollow laugh at the idea of being considered "prosperous"). I think, too, there must have been a little prick of unease at the realisation that there existed a lot of resentful and hungry men out there, united by common bitterness. They were, after all, entitled to be bitter. Seeing the old newsreels, one may wonder that undernourished and undervalued men could march such distances like soldiers. It was probably because many of them were old soldiers, reaping the rewards for their service from a government which didn't care.

There was unrest in other circles too. In the previous August, Mum, Mary and I had been in London, in Aldgate, waiting for a coach after a family visit. We had been struck by the groups of young men standing around eyeing other groups. These were the days when "Law and Order" was something we had perfect confidence in. So we didn't feel nervous and were rather surprised when an avuncular bobby came over and advised Mum to get us off the street as soon as possible, "just in case". The "trouble", of course, was Sir Oswald Mosley and his blackshirts (though they were not recognisable as such on this occasion; this was a sort of warming-up exercise). It was October before the "Battle of Cable Street" brought things to a head — but back on the Green we felt it couldn't possibly have any interest for us.

On the lighter side, a glimpse of the future was given us with the first television broadcast. There had been a brief and restricted showing at Olympia in August. This of course hardly touched our lives at all; our family didn't have a wireless set until four months after this event, and that was wonderful enough for us. In any case, few people were suggesting that the new invention was more than a novel toy for the idle rich. There was nothing to suggest that it would one day transform our lives.

Of course, it was in the late autumn of 1936 that speculation was rife about the King's love life, tactfully played down though it was till the bombshell of the Abdication. We — even, dimly, we children — knew that the King had always been considered a "bit of a lad". The public forgave him much — even rather liking him for his sins. He had been the world's most eligible bachelor for so long; Society mothers (as well as mothers from lower down the social scale) had dreamed of having him for a son-in-law. Debutantes and village maidens had his picture by their beds. The housemaid at the Rectory "wept buckets", Mary reported, when the news first broke that her idol had feet of clay.

None of this, I may say, was discussed in our house. As for the infamous Mrs Simpson, I can't recall that my mother ever spoke her name, and "divorce" was a word never uttered in my presence. I can't remember what the shock felt like, personally. I just remember sitting at our desks, staring at the wireless set (a recent gift from our governor) above the dais, the Headmaster staring at some point above our heads, looking solemn. Presumably this was the day after the announcement. At breaktime we chattered excitedly. I said, "Wouldn't

173

it be funny having a King Albert?" But of course, we didn't. And Mrs Simpson? How could anyone who had the whole world to choose from pick a woman of — what? — our mothers' age, a plain, dull, middle-aged woman, looking like a governess and always dressed in black. The reaction of most people seemed to be "Whatever does he see in her?" and a lot of plain, dull middle-aged women must have felt encouraged.

Just before Christmas that year (actually on Christmas Eve) came the great event of our lives; we acquired a wireless set of our own, hire-purchased from Curry's at one-and-six a week. Nothing ostentatious, of course; in fact, it was the least ostentatious set I ever saw in that era of Art Deco cabinets and fretwork sunbursts. "I told them I didn't want any of that tuppenny ha'penny rubbish," said my father (especially not at half-a-crown a week, he might have added). We had nothing by which to judge its performance (and in fact it proved to be an indifferent performer). No matter, for a while it was wonderful, an Open Sesame to a glamorous world of music and entertainment of which we had hitherto only caught tantalising glimpses, and at last I was able to enter into debates in the school playground, and keep abreast of all the latest songs, courtesy of Henry Hall and the B.B.C. Dance Orchestra. For a long time, Dad had insisted that the gramophone was a far superior piece of equipment (for we had quite a nice gramophone): "You could have what you wanted, when you wanted it, not at the whim of the B.B.C." When funds had permitted, he had bought sixpenny records from Woolworth's, some of them the excruciating "comedy" records of the period, "Cohen On the Phone" (no political correctness in those days!), "Leslie Fuller's Pleasure Cruise", "Sandy the Fireman" or ". . . Burglar" or ". . . Policeman" — how he laughed at those! (A mite too heartily?) These were trotted out to entertain the unwary guest, and when the guest expressed pleasure, he was likely to get a second helping.

But now, of course, the wireless was king. But not to be used with thoughtless abandon. There was no question of its forming a background to our lives. For a start, there was the accumulator to consider (that had to be taken down to the village for recharging), and batteries had to be saved up for. So we shopped around for our programmes, and sat listening carefully, so not to waste any of them. (There was girl down the round who claimed to be able to knit, read, and "listen in" to music at the same time; we considered this the height of sophistication.)

Down at the Rectory, early in the next year, Mary fell ill. At first it seemed little more than a cold, through which she continued on duty, but later she was getting chest pains and she was sent to bed. I went up to the little attic room during one lunch hour from school to take her some clean night things, and I was horrified at her depressing state. The room was cold and cheerless, and it was obvious that the rest of the staff had enough to do, in her absence, without running up and down stairs to wait on her. She got worse. The doctor advised that she should go home, something he should surely have done earlier. After two or three weeks of my mother's nursing she seemed better.

But it took a long time before she was "our Mary" again. Actually, she never was, quite, and I have no doubt that the seeds of the disease which was later to kill her were sown then. But, on the surface, she recovered and in due course was proclaimed fit to go back to work.

The cook at the Rectory had always seemed fond of Mary, and welcomed her back warmly (as well she might). I used to go to the Rectory after school on Guide evenings, to save me the walk home and then back again, and I would sit in the servants' parlour with a cup of tea and the cook would regale me with tales of her experiences below stairs. Among other things, she told me about her days in the service of the Bowes-Lyon family, and of the early life of the then Queen, whom she referred to as "Lizzie Lyon". "A proper little madam," said the cook.

As it turned out, all was not well with the cook herself; she began to have funny turns. Perhaps it was during one of these that Mary had to take over the cooking for an evening. It happened while the Rector and his wife were away, and Lady Phyll's parents, the Duke and Duchess of B., were "house-sitting". A meal had to be rustled up at short notice. Remembering her Cookery lessons at school, Mary produced a main course of "Cheese Dreams", recommended by the cookery teacher as, "a handy standby when the family is hungry and the cupboard is nearly bare." "Cheese Dreams" were, in fact, fried sandwiches of bread and cheese, which the Duke and Duchess solemnly ate, without comment.

No doubt they were relieved that the cook's indisposition didn't last long.

Things came to a head quite soon after that. One day, without warning, the cook chased Mary round the kitchen with a carving knife. Not much seems to have been known in those days about schizophrenia; "split personality" was treated either as a joke or as a subject for a good story; no one expected to have a "split personality" next door to them. I've no idea what happened to the cook, but I gather she was "locked up". My mother insisted on Mary's coming home. Lady Phyll was as nearly moved to tears as she could be, and begged Mum to reconsider, but that was out of the question.

For the next few months, Mary was either at home or taking on little short-term jobs, domestic or, for a spell, as postwoman, having acquired an old bike which she had painted blue (hailed by the local lads as the Blue Bird). Always interested in politics, she joined the Labour Party in the town, and at least once joined some publicity drive, touring the area on the back of a lorry.

Mr Britnell's job up North folded, and they returned to Pigotts, now with a little daughter who became a joy to us all, though she was as spirited as her mother. Jobs were hard to find, even for the educated, and the Britnells fell on hard times, things becoming so bad that once, when they were going on holiday (with me accompanying them, as I was recovering from whooping cough), my mother had to lend them some spending money as otherwise they would have been completely broke. The holiday was at one of the early holiday camps — but a far cry from Billy Butlin; this was a Civil Service holiday camp, with a "nice" clientele, and I felt a bit out of place.

The Britnells were middle-class intellectuals with some distinguished friends, some of whom came to visit. One, Patrick Balfour, later Lord Kinross, was a travel writer much concerned with the Middle East. He was a member of the Evelyn Waugh circle, and served as a fellow journalist in Ethiopia, on which *Scoop* is based. And he is thought to be the model for "Lord Balcain" in *Vile Bodies*. Mr Britnell (who many years later became a minor public figure himself) was, like my father, a Socialist, and they shared the publications of the Left Book Club. But of course, he saw the problems of "the workers" from a distance, even if poverty was a condition not unknown to him.

Mrs B. would have made a splendid Suffragette — if she hadn't been too tired for it, for her health fluctuated — conveniently, my mother opined. When she was on form, she had the stomach for a fight. There was a landowner who had put up a barricade to stop the locals using a path which, if not legally a right of way, had been used as such for all living memory. I recall a summer evening when Mrs B. and Mary took a wheelbarrow down the lane to where the offending barricade was, took it down and wheeled it home. They sat back and waited for the explosion, but rather disappointingly, none came, and as far as I know the obstacle was never replaced.

Mary was anxious to embark on some sort of career. Back at the Tye, she had first used a telephone and was intrigued by it. It's strange, now, to think that in the 1930s a great proportion of the population had never used a 'phone and were in awe of it. My mother was afraid of it all her life, and I don't think my father ever made a call. It happened at the Tye on one occasion that a neighbour wanted to let her sister know that she had just given birth. The sister lived eight miles away, and, incredibly, had access to a 'phone. My mother was thrown into a state of terror when asked to make the call, declaring that her hearing wasn't good enough (not true — though certainly the lines were not always as clear as those we take for granted now). Mary volunteered enthusiastically — she was always keen on new experiences.

In those days, I don't think public call boxes were a feature of the countryside, but in most places there would be one house with a blue enamel sign outside saying, "You May Telephone From Here". At the Tye, "Here" was the Northwoods, and it was to Mrs Northwood that Mary repaired clutching our neighbour's tuppence. Afterwards, we wanted to know all the details. "A voice says: 'Number please!' and you say the number you want, and then she says: 'You're thrrrough!' and then the person at the other end says: 'Hullo?'" This was riveting stuff, and she basked in the glory of it, deciding there and then to become a telephonist.

When we moved to Pigotts, incredibly we became the "Here" from which calls could be made. Though in fact I only remember one customer, when one of the newcomers to the Green was in urgent need of the District Nurse. The telephone, one of the old, wall-fitting kind with the receiver hanging at the side, was in the middle "parlour" which was almost never used. My parents transmitted their fear of it so successfully that it was years before I was at ease with the instrument. I think they had visions of me getting the hang of the thing and running up huge bills — but as no-one in my circle had a phone, it seems unlikely.

Once, when my parents were out and I was in the room with my friend Cissie, she dared me to touch it. I wouldn't, for my parents had said that if I did the police would come. She jeered at this (understandably) and gave the earpiece a little shove. I was thrown into a blind panic, rushing out of the house hysterically, straining my ears for the sound of the approaching police car (interestingly, it was a car that I expected, though our local policemen, who I knew quite well, only had bikes; presumably I thought the enormity of my crime called for something more dramatic).

But poor Mum was hoist on her own petard when, later, a 'phone call became necessary. We were alone in the house, so she buttered me up with encouraging phrases: "You can hear better than me," etc. I was thrown in at the deep end, for it was a "trunks", and the operator repeated the number I gave with a scornfully correct intonation, and the connection was a poor one, and when I got through, I was hardly coherent as I gave my message. All this, when by that time I had a telephonist sister.

It was no small thing for an elementary school girl to get into a Post Office job, which carried with it considerable prestige, for it spelled Security, that greatest of assets. Mary's c.v. didn't look too promising, for kitchen maids had little in common with Civil Servants. But her references were glowing when it came to honesty, hard work, and general integrity. There were family conferences.

"What shall I put where it says: 'Reason for leaving'?" she asked.

" 'To better myself'," said Mum firmly.

"Being out of work is hardly bettering herself," I pointed out, thinking how surprised they would be at the Head Office if she put: "Cook tried to murder me" — but what better reason could there be?

She was sent an appointment for an interview, at Clerkenwell. Mum went with her. On the way Mary bought a new coat for the occasion, and a hat — a little black fez, a style which had become fashionable because of the wedding of King Farouk of Egypt, on whom Mary had a crush. She passed ("scraped through") the written test — and indeed, Mary's spelling wasn't a strong point — but where she shone was in the vocal test. She had always had a sweet, clear voice, both in singing and speech, and perhaps it was that that clinched it. (Later, she won an elocution prize — and this in competition with Grammar school girls and the like.) And of course, she interviewed well. People liked Mary. The Post Office was very proud of its "Golden Voiced Girls"; it was almost in the area of being a "glamour" profession. She was engaged to start training. But there was a wait for a place, and we made the most of having her at home with us while we could.

I can't remember when we saw our first searchlight. It was probably in the summer of 1937, or the early autumn.

There was a field about two miles down the lane where we used to walk, en famille, at summer weekends to watch the air displays — two or three little biplanes which used to do stunts and, I believe, offered short trips for five shillings (Mary would have loved one, but Mum wouldn't let her). I remember a tiny red-and-white-check plane on the wings of which a girl used to stand as it flew. I suppose she was strapped on pretty well. (We watched from the road, thus avoiding the admission charge.)

Somewhere between the summer of 1937 and 1938, the R.A.F. took over the field opposite the little improvised airstrip, a narrow field with woods on one side and the country lane on the other. Perhaps there were searchlights tucked away there somewhere. All we knew was that, without any prior rumour, they were there, sweeping across the sky as it grew dark. A little shiver ran through me, overshadowed as I had always been by my parents' wartime reminiscences.

"It's just summer manoeuvres," my mother said. "They're just practising." Practising? For what?

But the new development had its lighter side. Searchlights were operated by young men, young men in uniform, moreover. The local girls found this very interesting. I blush to admit that we — well, Mary and friends, really, for I was too young to be more than an interested observer — were not immune, and there were times when our healthy country walks had a tendency to pass that way, and the odd whistle was, to Mary perhaps more than most, a welcome morale-boost, for she was genuinely convinced she was ugly. Mum wasn't too happy about the new development.

The little "stunt" biplanes came no more and in their place were equally fragile machines, Lysanders, which were to play a part, later, in the work of the Secret Services. For some of these heroes and heroines (of whom we knew nothing, of course, for many years) their last glimpse of England must have been of our little lane, and the woods, and the scene of our summer afternoon saunters.

One September afternoon we were called out of school, lined up in the playground and fitted with gasmasks. It was too unreal to be frightening. Some of the children actually found it exciting. For myself, I just recall the smell of hot rubber, and hating the shut-in feeling.

At home, discussion was under way about what was going to happen to the little ones. Little Janet could perhaps have a mask, but the new baby (for the Britnells had recently been blessed with a son) would have to be put in a bath with a damp blanket over him. Mrs Britnell declared that if there was no provision for her child, they knew what they could do with her own gasmask.

For a few days I switched off all feeling. School became quite bearable because we were united in uncertainty. And then, suddenly, miraculously, it was all over, and the Prime Minister, Neville Chamberlain, was the hero of the hour, with his "piece of paper" which was supposed to spell "Peace in our time".

Mary had finished her training by this time, and had been posted to the Victoria Exchange, thus being very near the centre of all the excitement. ". . . I'm in my seventh heaven this week. I'm in the section that has lines to every Cabinet Minister, Foreign, War, Home, Agric., Labour and Admiralty . . . A girl from the Foreign Office rang and said the Cabinet had just risen, and she thought I'd like to know . . . I feel I'm in a glorious dream."

She had reported on the digging of trenches in all the parks, and the Exchange being blacked out, "even the lavatories". Now, with the danger apparently passed, one got the feeling she was almost disappointed.

She wasn't having things easy. She was lodging with Cousin May in a crowded but easy-going household at Acton. Her income while training was twelve and sixpence a week, of which she gave May five shillings (she had offered more). Of the rest, she had fares and "lunches" to pay — though one suspects these were very frugal. Once she was faced with only a penny ha'penny for her homeward ride, and had to use her "lucky" threepenny bit, kept in reserve and to double as a substitute suspender "button" in an emergency. Even with that, she had to walk part of the way — and went in the wrong direction! With all of that, she kept cheerful. Every new experience was a delight, and she was learning her way around, even occasionally going to the theatre (but that was after her move to Victoria, when her salary rose to fifteen shillings with additions when she did overtime, which was as often as possible). She was learning, too, to be a modern woman. She acquired an uplift brassiere (necessary in her case, but considered a great bit of self-indulgence). And with the burgeoning of "modern" women's magazines, full of advice and glowing advertisements, she was able to keep abreast of all that was new in the world of "glamour" and sophistication — a word which began to figure largely in her vocabulary. Living with our relations, she had a fairly lively social life, but mostly within the family circle. I only once heard mention of a dance, and that was a Labour affair, and the only partner she mentioned was a young man who smelled of fish paste.

CHAPTER
SEVEN

Over the River

"Over the river and into the trees . . ."

We left Pigotts that autumn. The Britnells continued to have money problems which had finally come to the point where only the sale of the house and a move to something cheaper would save them — this despite the fact that Mrs B. had, most unusually for those days, gone back to work and travelled up to town every day, leaving Mr B. in charge of the little ones.

We scoured the local papers for somewhere to live. One day, when Mum and I were in the town killing time till our bus home, I saw an advertisement in an estate agent's window. It was for a little bungalow, on the surface quite neat and modern, on offer at twelve-and-six a week. We obtained the key, and Dad biked over to view it the following Sunday. On being questioned eagerly on his return, he would only say, "It needs just a bit of attention". Knowing Dad's phraseology, we should have feared the worst, for his comments were, to say the least, an understatement. It was, for a start, the very tiniest bungalow I have ever seen. It did have an inside tap, and electric light (with lethal wiring) and a gas stove of great antiquity. And everywhere that rust could be established, it was. There was a very long, unkempt garden, and (of course) no fence or gate — I knew by now we were destined never to have those. To describe the place as "jerrybuilt" is perhaps to insult Jerry.

The small town on the edge of which Oakdene was situated (there was, of course, no oak tree for miles) was at that time a community of perhaps two thousand, but that it was a "town" at all (for it had an Urban District Council) excited me. It had two of the requisites for urban living: a fish and chip shop and a cinema. This last must have been one of the first outside the big towns, and indeed, I've since discovered it was in business before the Great War and it had a frontage like the Alamo. There was a half hourly bus service, and a Green Line coach on the hour to London. And we ourselves lived seven minutes (five, if you ran) from a main line station. The years ahead seemed full of promise.

I still had about six weeks of schooling left to go. In the event, they were the happiest of my school life. The Head, Miss Burnet, a sober-looking Jane Eyre of a woman, restored the confidence that Mr and Mrs L. between them had done their best to destroy (yet strangely, she told me later that the report from my previous school had been very good. Perhaps, now that he was getting rid of me, Mr L. felt he could be generous). "If only I'd had you earlier," Miss Burnet said. But I think she was overestimating my capabilities. I really just wanted to get through life as comfortably as possible, and be beautiful, and loved. All the same, it was a bit disturbing to be seen as a lost cause at fourteen!

My working future became a subject for discussion. Jobs were still hard to come by, except, as ever, in domestic service. There was a time, perhaps only a year or two earlier, when this would have been the obvious choice for the likes of me — though surely no one in the world could have been a more unlikely candidate. Once, at the Tye, when one of the visiting gentlewomen had said to me that I would make a good parlourmaid (I was "tall, and spoke and moved nicely," she said) I was not displeased. The parlourmaids I had seen in films looked pretty in their lacy caps and aprons, and I quite liked the thought of moving amongst beautiful furniture and delicate china. Besides which, as I planned at that time to marry into the aristocracy, it seemed a promising first step. But Mary's experience had altered my parents' view of service as a career, and my mother no longer was heard to say that "hard work never killed anyone".

Nothing had come along by the Christmas holiday, so I went back to school afterwards, to Miss Burnet's approval and my own satisfaction. Although I longed for the bit of freedom which in theory would come with my emergence from the classroom, I was in no hurry to join the "real" world, which I had come to suspect was an uncomfortable place and probably boring. Yet when the manager of a local grocery store came to the school in search of a trainee cashier, I allowed my name to go forward.

The Stores was a branch of a very small chain of grocers; "chain" gives a misleading impression, for there were only two other shops in other small towns. Our local branch was situated in an old 16th century building, previously an inn (inns were obviously built to last). It smelled delicious, as grocers always did. There was a Provisions counter on the right as you entered, with a marble top and great mounds of butter which were slapped and patted into shape between wooden boards, then weighed and wrapped; there were massive hams, and the cheeses were cut with a wire to suit individual requirements, and you could sample a sliver before you made your choice. On the opposite counter were Groceries, and that included all the spices of Araby and teas from various parts of the Orient, and different kinds of loose coffee (though the less important customers were catered for by the provision of Camp in bottles, but these were tucked away for they were thought to lower the tone, and such customers were served rather condescendingly). And in the darker recesses of the shop were wines and spirits, dispensed by the Shop Manager himself, with much bowing and scraping if the social position of the customer appeared to merit it. The General Manager, a strange, taciturn bachelor who lived more or less above the shop, and was (like our old Green landlord) a Plymouth Brother, had interviewed me in the chilly hall of his quarters. The interview consisted of asking me to write my name and add up a column of figures. The job was then mine. I saw my mother hesitate when the wage was mentioned — seven and six for a week which was to average forty-five hours (and once, fifty, because on Fridays and Saturdays, when most people did their shopping and paid their bills, I was still cashing up and trying to balance the books after the rest of the staff had gone). And of course, unlike domestic service, there was no "all found", so it wasn't a princely wage by any standard. But I found myself accepting; I felt I'd come too far to go back.

The store had a Drapery department, entered separately, with two long counters, and bales of wonderful-smelling materials and dressmaker's busts of Edwardian proportions, coyly draped with lace collars and georgette scarves. At the rear of the shop, up some steps and under an arch, there was a section where corsets and underwear and even more intimate items could be purchased. The corsetry looked as though it had been there since the death of Queen Alexandra, and I can honestly believe that it had, for it had a musty, moth-bally smell and the rigidity of a bygone age. I never saw anyone buying it. The department was presided over by an old-young woman, probably no more than twenty-five, but middle-aged in her gait and demeanour, with her hair in neat marcel waves and dressed in neat navy blue or what in those days was unashamedly called "nigger". This lady wore an engagement ring, and I couldn't help noticing that the acquisition of one of these made people treat you more respectfully. It struck me that to be engaged was a state devoutly to be wished.

In all departments there were, of course, the high round chairs found in most shops then, and customers were treated almost reverently, always called "madam" (few "sirs" shopped for groceries). This might be omitted if the customer was well-known to the assistant, but even then, the tone used would be quite different to that used elsewhere. Above the counters were the wooden or metal cups into which the money and the ticket were placed when the purchase was completed. A handle was then pulled and the cup would go whirring across the shop and disappear through a hole high up in the wall, ending up in what was really rather like a little ski-lift terminus, above a high, old-fashioned desk of the kind seen in Dickens illustrations. This was my domain.

When I think of the frugal staffing in the big modern supermarkets, I marvel at the number of employees it took to run a small-town grocers in those pre-war days. In addition to the counter staff of about six, there were two or three men in the stock room besides the Shop Manager, and three girls in the office including myself, plus the General Manager, who rarely appeared in public. Two of the stockroom men were also van drivers who delivered orders to outlying villages, orders which had been collected earlier in the week by two older men who rode out on bicycles. Then there was a gangling youth of about my own age who delivered in the town, on his tradesman's bike. He, poor lad, imagined himself in love with me (it was Stanley all over again). He would find excuses to come into the office and linger, gazing wordlessly, to my cringing embarrassment and the hilarity of the rest of the staff. When he started lying in wait for me at the end of the day, I felt it was time to be cruel to be kind, and eventually he got the message. Anxious though I was to be the object of some man's undying love, I felt that at fourteen I was a bit young to settle for the likes of Cyril.

But the real bane of my life at the Stores was the Shop Manager, Mr Turnbull. The dislike was obviously mutual, for he could never resist getting in little digs, and I actually felt quite ill in his presence. He had a rushing, noiseless sort of walk, and a rapid way of talking with which his teeth never quite caught up. I got the impression that he thought I was too big for my boots. The office girls felt (or behaved as though they felt) a cut above the counter staff, and the latter tended to treat me with a sort of chilly awkwardness, not knowing where to place me.

Mr Turnbull had got my measure much earlier, while I was still at school. My mother had asked me to go, in my dinner break, to buy a block of salt. She gave me a penny. "What if it's tuppence?" I said. "It won't be," she said firmly. (I later learned that a penny was all she had.) But the salt was indeed tuppence, and it was this man who had served me, when I had to confess I had only a penny — and this in front of my new school friends, and in a nearly empty shop, so that every assistant witnessed my shame. I vowed never to go in that shop again, and in the event could only do so by convincing myself that I was too insignificant for anyone to remember. But the odious Mr Turnbull remembered, you may depend, and never let me forget, in little subtle, spiteful ways, that he remembered. And that being so, he resented my talking "posh" — i.e., I didn't have the local accent, as he reasoned I should have done.

One day in the Spring of that year, a lady called at our house to see how many rooms we had. This was to see if we would be able to take any evacuees, should there be a war. "Purely a precautionary measure," she said in her bright Social Worker voice. "Better be safe than sorry."

Of course there was no question of our being able to take any one; we barely had room for ourselves. Anyway, Mary would be coming home. I think this was our parents' decision rather than her own, but she went along with it. She got transferred to the nearest exchange, about five miles away, and bought herself a bike at half-a-crown a week to do the journey, hoping thus to save her train fare and slim her legs.

Our social life wasn't hectic, but we sometimes went over to a neighbour who had a large family and gave little impromptu dances, sometimes on a Sunday night (and it's a measure of my mother's increasingly relaxed attitude in these matters that she raised no objections). I fell in love once or twice, and was fallen in love with, but it was many years before the two things came together. The whole subject worried me a bit, and I got fidgety when my friends discussed it. A girl down the road worked in a bookshop, and she got hold of various books reputed to be "hot", and used to read extracts which made us giggle, and then she bought — quite openly, and we marvelled at her nerve — *The Psychology of Sex*, which I would recognise now as a classic but very dull work. She read to us from this, pronouncing it "Physiology . . ." (we didn't know what that meant, either). We didn't understand a word, confirming my unvoiced opinion that the less one knew about such things the better.

Earlier, my cousin Joan had been friendly with a young man, a German student, over on holiday, and they had corresponded when he went home. When Joan got engaged, she passed on the pen-friendship to Mary, and for a few months Fritz and Mary exchanged letters and photos. Fritz was very handsome, very Aryan — very Hitler-youth, I see now. He joined the Luftwaffe, and his letters became full of enthusiasm for it. At the beginning of August, Mary's last letter was returned by the Post Office.

As the summer wore on, I felt less and less well, and Mum decided I should give up my job and have a rest. This, despite the fact that my five shillings contribution to the housekeeping was valued, for my father was on short time, no-one wanting to have their houses painted until they knew what the future held.

I must have seen August out at the shop, hot and weary. (I heard someone on the radio recently declaring that 1939 was a bad summer; my memory says otherwise, as does the memory of a writer who said, "It was a wonderful summer, the best for years . . .")

Earlier, I had started digging a hole for a lily pond in the back garden. Now I found enough energy to enlarge it and turn it into an air raid shelter (for we just came outside the boundary within which we would have qualified for an Anderson). The digging was heavy going, in view of my declining health, but I was

194

reasonably satisfied with the result. My father put the finishing touches, covering it with planks and turf, and inside I fashioned a seat out of the yellow clay. It reminded me horribly of a newly-dug grave, and I didn't like the worms.

At work in that last week, our two van drivers were called up for the Army, for they were Territorials. Suddenly everyone was being very nice to them — even nice to each other, with gloomy recollections of "the last lot". Even the odious Mr Turnbull forgot to be horrid. (I should add that neither of our would-be heroes lasted long; Norman was found to have a weak heart and was released from service, and George, who had been something of a womaniser, died a few weeks later when a tent pole fell on him in Northern Ireland. He was deeply mourned by a young woman who continued to put a memoriam notice in the paper well into the 1970s. Remembering his philandering ways, I hope she didn't let his loss condemn her to a lifetime of spinsterhood.)

Coming home from work on that last day, I felt overwhelmingly that I was coming to the end of an era. I'd left my job, and had no idea where and when I should get another. I crossed the bridge (which was the county boundary at that point) and I thought of a bit of poetry — Longfellow, I think — about ". . . Standing with reluctant feet, Where the brook and river meet . . .", an hilariously outdated view of maidenly adolescence, even in 1939! But the mixture of excitement and fear it sums up hasn't, even now, quite lost its relevance.

I got to the station and waited for the crossing gates to open. The evacuee trains were coming through; long, slow trains they were. At this stage, they weren't stopping at our station, although at thirty miles' distance from London we were considered "safe" (later, this was proved an illusion). By the time the trains got this far, the children's excitement had begun to wear off; seeing cows and fields for the first time was no longer a novelty. Some of them stood at the windows in a listless fashion as though the enormity of what was happening to them was too much to take in. Here and there one of them would wave a handkerchief or a little Union Jack, but without enthusiasm, and I waved back, feeling that it was all too unreal to be really sad.

We were advised not to travel, and warned that if we did so we could be subject to much inconvenience, for all the lines out of London would be clogged with evacuees. Taking ourselves off to London to my cousin Joan's wedding on the Saturday in spite of this, we actually had no trouble. (No one, of course, was travelling into London.) Joan's family — she was the daughter of my mother's elder sister, who had married rather comfortably — had pulled out the stops to give her a "proper" wedding with all the trimmings. The looming crisis had thrown a spanner into the works. Few out-of-town guests had been able, or prepared to risk, making the journey. All the waiters at the hotel where the reception was to be held had been called up.

In the event, it was a nice, cosy, family affair, at home, with masses of lovely food intended for many more than were present, and we younger members of the party were encouraged to stuff ourselves, and we did (the memory of that food came back to me, mouth-wateringly, in the lean years to come). The bridal pair left for a night in a West End hotel (the cost of which was a pound each). We ourselves stayed overnight with my aunt so that we were all together when the British ultimatum to Germany ran out, at eleven o'clock the following morning. We were told to stand by our wireless sets, and I have a feeling there may have been some appropriately sombre music, filling the gap. To offset that, perhaps, I sat on the stairs, blowing a toy trumpet — left over from the wedding celebrations, I suppose — and "playing" "Deep Purple", which I can never hear now without recalling those eerie moments. The minutes ticked away, and at 11.15a.m. the Prime Minister came on to say his piece, ending with, ". . . and that consequently this country is at war with Germany."

It was almost an anti-climax. I can't remember my feelings — awe, I suppose, in the face of such a momentous occasion; numbness, because I didn't dare to let myself think. There seemed to be quite a crowd in the house by this time. They stood quietly, just staring at the wireless. Aunt Ede sobbed. Someone — one of the men — said, "That's it, then." When conversation restarted, it was in muted tones, as if we were in church.

My teenage cousin Reg, Mary and I went for a walk, glad to get away from the gloomy adults. We talked of how our lives would now change. Reg said he'd join the Air Force. Mary, in a dress with a pattern of petunias, looked tired and pale, but she too found the future exciting, and her eyes were bright.

We walked in the park, where the petunias matched Mary's dress. Then the air raid siren sounded, the long rising and falling, heart-lurching wail which was to become all too familiar. But we weren't worried because there had been several practice runs lately and we didn't doubt that this was one of those. However, when we turned our steps homeward and came in sight of Aunt's gate, we saw them all gathered, waving wildly and shouting at us. It was for real — though, as it turned out, actually a false alarm, a rehearsal, one might say, for things to come. But it had been the first indication that this war was going to be different, and we were all in the firing line.

And with a lifetime of dread behind me, I made an extraordinary discovery. I wasn't afraid.

Also available in ISIS Large Print:

A Midhurst Lad

Ronald E. Boxall

Although poverty and illness marred his young life, the author's sense of mischief and humour shine through this charming childhood autobiography.

Born into the Boxall family in 1924, Ronald was brought up in Duck Lane, Midhurst, at that time an address synonymous with hardship. The tale of "the average life of an average boy born of poor parents, who lived under slum conditions, yet dwelt in the centre of a tiny and pretty town set in a near paradise of pastoral and sylvan delights". Ronald tells his story with natural wit and clarity, sharing his memories of a bygone age.

ISBN 0-7531-9320-5 (hb)
ISBN 0-7531-9321-3 (pb)

Sing a Song of Sixpence

Hazel Wheeler

A collection of tales of life in Yorkshire during the 1920s and 1930s, which include accounts of the pandemonium caused by a fire alarm in a crowded cinema, a poor family moving house, celebrations for the coronations of George VI and Elizabeth II, ice-cream made of potatoes during the war, scarlet fever and bonfire nights.

ISBN 0-7531-9328-0 **(hb)**
ISBN 0-7531-9329-9 **(pb)**